8 LESSONS IN MILITARY LEADERSHIP
for Entrepreneurs

BY ROBERT T. KIYOSAKI

8 LESSONS IN MILITARY LEADERSHIP

for Entrepreneurs

By Robert T. Kiyosaki

PLATA®
PUBLISHING

Published by Plata Publishing, LLC

CASHFLOW, Rich Dad, B-I Triangle, and CASHFLOW Quadrant are registered trademarks of CASHFLOW Technologies, Inc.

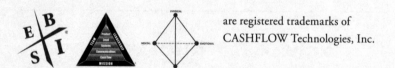

are registered trademarks of
CASHFLOW Technologies, Inc.

Plata Publishing, LLC
4330 N. Civic Center Plaza
Suite 100
Scottsdale, AZ 85251
(480) 998-6971

Visit our websites: PlataPublishing.com and RichDad.com
Printed in the United States of America

First Edition: May 2015
ISBN: 978-1-61268-053-8

Best-selling Books
by Robert T. Kiyosaki

Rich Dad Poor Dad
What the Rich Teach Their Kids About Money –
That the Poor and Middle Class Do Not

Rich Dad's CASHFLOW Quadrant
Guide to Financial Freedom

Rich Dad's Guide to Investing
What the Rich Invest in That the Poor and Middle Class Do Not

Rich Dad's Rich Kid Smart Kid
Give Your Child a Financial Head Start

Rich Dad's Retire Young Retire Rich
How to Get Rich and Stay Rich

Rich Dad's Prophecy
Why the Biggest Stock Market Crash in History Is Still Coming…
And How You Can Prepare Yourself and Profit from It!

Rich Dad's Success Stories
Real-Life Success Stories from Real-Life People
Who Followed the Rich Dad Lessons

Rich Dad's Guide to Becoming Rich
Without Cutting Up Your Credit Cards
Turn Bad Debt into Good Debt

Rich Dad's Who Took My Money?
Why Slow Investors Lose and Fast Money Wins!

Rich Dad Poor Dad for Teens
The Secrets About Money—That You Don't Learn In School!

Escape the Rat Race
Learn How Money Works and Become a Rich Kid

Rich Dad's Before You Quit Your Job
Ten Real-Life Lessons Every Entrepreneur Should Know
About Building a Multimillion-Dollar Business

Rich Dad's Increase Your Financial IQ
Get Smarter with Your Money

Robert Kiyosaki's Conspiracy of the Rich
The 8 New Rules of Money

Unfair Advantage
The Power of Financial Education

Why "A" Students Work for "C" Students
Rich Dad's Guide to Financial Education for Parents

Second Chance
for Your Money, Your Life and Our World

*To the men and women
who serve in the armed forces
all over the world*

Our Million-Book Mission

... and what it can mean to you

The Rich Dad Company and Plata Publishing
will make a generous contribution for every copy of this book
sold between its release date and April 8, 2017
to provide funding for programs and projects
that support servicemen and women
and their families around the world.

We are committed to selling 1 million copies of this book
and know that the funds we distribute
as a result of those sales will help
to serve and support our brothers and sisters in the military...
active duty, retired, or in the reserves.

To learn more about how you can support or benefit
from this Mission visit
RichDad.com/MillionBookMission

Oath of Enlistment

I do solemnly swear

that I will support and defend

the Constitution of the United States

against all enemies, foreign and domestic;

that I will bear true faith and allegiance to the same;

and that I will obey the orders

of the President of the United States

and the orders of the officers appointed over me,

according to regulations and the Uniform Code of Military Justice.

So help me God.

FOREWORD

by Lieutenant General Jack Bergman
United States Marine Corps, Retired

Quite possibly, the truest test for determining how well leaders have prepared those under their charge to perform would be for the leader to suddenly disappear and then evaluate how well those remaining continued to perform.

I am guessing that most leaders would prefer not to have such a radical situation occur. Well, in real life, 'stuff happens.' As was stated in the 2012 movie *Redtails*: "Experience is a cruel teacher; gives the exam first, then the lesson."

Relevant leaders put themselves last and everyone else first. Proactive leaders prepare individually and collectively to attain the best possible results under the worst possible conditions. Education and training followed by evaluation and more training culminating in execution is a never-ending cycle required for success.

As a 14-year-old Boy Scout, I was given the best leadership guidance EVER by another Scout who was immediately senior to me. In assigning my objectives for a two-week camp, he matter-of-factly stated, "Life is not a popularity contest. Go out there and get the job done."

In real life, simply "getting the job done" does not qualify an individual as a leader. Today's and, more importantly, tomorrow's leaders must have vision, adaptability, and grit in order to succeed in a digital world filled with analog humans. However, one essential element never changes. Lead by example!

Robert and I have been friends for over 40 years. We were roommates on board the ship that's pictured on the cover of this book. He writes with the passion of a young Marine officer and the wisdom of a seasoned, savvy, successful entrepreneur. And, while we disagree on some things, we wholeheartedly agree that 'those who quit never succeed' and that ongoing education is essential to success!

Enjoy the book and remember: Truly outstanding leadership is not about YOU, it is about ME. Morals and Ethics, that is.

Semper Fidelis,
Jack Bergman
Lieutenant General (Ret),
United States Marine Corps

CONTENTS

SPECIAL THANKS

There are two important contributors to this book that I want to introduce and acknowledge. They are Robb LeCount and Dave Leong.

Both men have served their country in the U.S. military, both joined the Rich Dad team in 2009, and both have embraced entrepreneurship on their path to financial freedom.

Robb, a former Navy Aviation Machinist Mate, plays a huge role in how The Rich Dad Company communications with the world in his role as Director of Information Technology at our company. He's also a real estate investor and the owner of multiple businesses, including a software testing company, and is working to create a line of health bars.

You'll find **Robb's Report** at the end of each chapter in this book. In those sections he'll share his thoughts on that chapter's content as well as some of his personal experiences from his years in the service.

Robb is also responsible for the Bonus Section you'll find at the end of this book: **Special Report on V.A. Loans.** He is passionate about the value that vets have in their V.A. Loan benefits and has taken the time to write and teach about what he's learned.

Robb is a student of Rich Dad Coaching and Rich Dad Education, has played a pivotal role in bringing the Rich Dad games and books— *CASHFLOW 101, CASHFLOW for Kids, Rich Dad Poor Dad* via CLUTCH, *CASHFLOW Classic* and *Capital City*—into the digital world via apps and digital learning platforms.

Apart from being a Navy squid… he's a natural leader and a huge asset to our Rich Dad team. And I thank him for his many contributions to this book.

Dave Leong attended the U.S. Air Force Academy in Colorado Springs, Colorado, graduated in 2004, and served as a First Lieutenant at Balad Airbase, Iraq. Dave has worked in several departments of The Rich Dad Company and today is the Marketing Manager for the Mobile Apps division. He continues to apply what he's learned to building his coffee shop, his online businesses, and investing in real estate.

If you've read other Rich Dad books, you know that I often write about Blair Singer, a Rich Dad Advisor, and his book *Team Code of Honor*. The military has an honor code and when I left the military one of the toughest transitions for me—from military to civilian life—was related to honor and code or, better said, the lack of it. I asked Dave to write about his experience with the Honor Code at the Air Force Academy, time in service, and how he's applying it now in the civilian world. You'll find his piece on Honor Code at the end of this book.

I know you'll find that the contributions from these two men reflect the values and the lessons they learned from the military and how they've applied them to their lives today. I thank them both—for their service and for being willing to share and teach what they've learned.

TRAINING FOR LIFE

I served in the Marine Corps during the Vietnam era. But I wasn't a career officer and didn't retire from the Marine Corps. I was able to retire, at age 47, because I had income coming in from my businesses and my investments. I did not have income from a career or a job.

I'm sure there are quite a few people who have been able to accomplish this, but I was able to do it in large part, due to my military training.

I loved military flight school because we were inspired to face our fears every day. I was not in flight school for a steady paycheck or early retirement benefits, although I knew many student pilots who were. Career Marines are employees of the U.S. government.

I was in the Marine Corps and flight school for the inspiration, and preparation, for war. Rather than seek security, our instructors forced us to practice "emergency maneuvers" on each and every flight. Rather than hope and pray things would go right, the instructors would intentionally cripple the aircraft in some way, sometimes even killing the engine. They forced us to face our fears, keep our cool— and still fly the aircraft. It was perfect training for a life in business.

Many people will struggle financially simply because their emotions run their lives. Rather than face their financial fears, they hide from them. Many employees hide under the blanket of a steady paycheck and job security.

I joined the Marine Corps to fight for capitalism and against communism, but when I retuned from Vietnam I came home to find an America with a dying spirit and a growing entitlement mentality.

I found more communists here in America than on the fields of Vietnam.

I am writing this book to turn America around. If anyone can save America it is those who have sworn to protect her and have fought for her. It's not just our duty, it's what we are trained to do.

This book will show you that the eight principles of our military training are the same principles that are essential for being a successful entrepreneur. The men and women in the military have incredibly strong spirit. It is our spirit that will turn our country around and return us to the capitalism that is the foundation of our country.

Part One

A CALL TO DUTY

Chapter One

MISSION CRITICAL

It breaks my heart to read about veterans returning from the Iraq and Afghanistan, unable to find jobs.

It breaks my heart to see young veterans, wounded warriors, facing the rest of their lives without legs, arms, or handicapped in other ways.

It breaks my heart to give a few dollars to a fellow Vietnam era veteran, standing on a corner, head bowed, asking for food or money.

And it breaks my heart that many military families are on Food Stamps and other government support because they do not earn a living wage.

The Need for Entrepreneurs

This book is written for anyone who is an entrepreneur, or dreams of becoming an entrepreneur one day.

This book is also written for men and women who are serving—or who have served—in the armed services because they have already gone through a unique and rigorous educational process, a process that's essential for all entrepreneurs.

As you may know, nine out of 10 new businesses fail within the first five years. Of the one in 10 that survives those first five years, nine out of 10 of those 'survivors' fail in the second five years.

The primary reason why most new entrepreneurs fail is simply because they lack the core *training*, the core *strengths* they need to withstand the rigors of being an entrepreneur. Some people call it *guts*. Others call it *perseverance*. In the military, it might be put this way: "Stand up, get off your butt, stop feeling sorry for yourself, stop pouting, stop sucking your thumb, and get going again. Your mama is ashamed of you—because your mama is tougher than you are." I think you get the point here.

Another important reason why most entrepreneurs fail is because our educational system trains people to be *employees*, not *entrepreneurs*. The world of an employee is very different from the world of an entrepreneur. One big difference is the concept of *paychecks*. If an employee does not receive his or her "paycheck" they quit and go looking for a new job". Most entrepreneurs must be tough enough to operate, sometimes for years, without a "paycheck."

In the world of 'small business,' sometimes called "mom-and-pop businesses," the entrepreneurs often earn less per hour than their employees, when the total number of work hours is taken into consideration. In most small businesses, the entrepreneur's most important work is done when the business is closed for the day. It is called *paperwork*... and addresses the behind-the-scenes jobs that keep a business running—like compliance requirements, invoicing and collection, accounting, and taxes.

When employees go on vacation, they can leave their work behind. When entrepreneurs go on vacation, the business goes with them.

If the business struggles or comes crashing down, an employee can walk away and look for a new job. The entrepreneur's work, at that point, is just beginning. When a business collapses, it's like digging yourself out of the rubble of a building brought down by an air strike. The damage, carnage, liabilities, and litigation can bury an entrepreneur for years. Many never recover, suffering from a business version of PTSD, Post Traumatic Stress Disorder.

Many 'experts' say, "Entrepreneurs fail because they are *under capitalized*." This means they do not have enough money—or access to money—to keep the business afloat. This fear of being "under capitalized," this lack of money as well as the absence of a steady paycheck, is what keeps most people clinging to job security as an employee.

I take a different position. In my opinion, it's not a lack of *capital*, it's a lack of entrepreneurial education, real-world business experience, and guts. If you talk with successful entrepreneurs, they will tell you they are always "under capitalized." They never have enough money to meet all the financial obligations required as an entrepreneur, let alone the capital needed to grow their business. Yet, somehow, true entrepreneurs keep going. Then one day, for some entrepreneurs, the money starts pouring in. It may take years. And I always find it amusing when I hear people say, "Oh, she was lucky." Or "They're an *overnight success*." Few know or appreciate the real story behind entrepreneurial successes.

This is why I believe men and women in the military have the unique core strengths and training to be entrepreneurs. In many cases, you have been trained to "do the impossible." Most college graduates are trained only to "find a job."

The character differences between those who have been trained to do the impossible—those willing to pay the price that's often called the *ultimate sacrifice*—are in sharp contrast to a person who has been trained to "look for a high-paying job with good benefits."

My military career began at the U.S. Merchant Marine Academy at Kings Point in New York, considered to be one of the top schools for leadership in the world. In 1965, I received Congressional nominations to both the U.S. Naval Academy and the U.S. Merchant Marine Academy from U.S. Senator and Medal of Honor recipient, Daniel K. Inouye.

I accepted an appointment to Kings Point. The school's mission is to train leaders for the Maritime Industry and graduates can be found working in ports and harbor operations all over the world, as captains of passenger liners, cargo ships, container ships, oil tankers, and ocean-going barges. A few graduates, like myself, opted to serve in the U.S. Navy, the Marine Corps, and the Coast Guard.

A graduate of Kings Point has the same pedigree in the Maritime and Shipping Industry as a West Pointer has in the U.S. Army. When I graduated in 1969, Kings Pointers were among the highest paid graduates in the world. That's because, although a military academy, the Academy was under the direction of the Department of Commerce, not the Department of Defense.

After graduating from Kings Point, I was accepted to U.S. Navy Flight School in Pensacola, Florida and flew for the U.S. Marine Corps in Vietnam. I am quite certain that if not for my military training, I wouldn't have made it as an entrepreneur.

What Is Cheating?

In traditional schools we're trained to take tests on our own. If you cooperate at test time, it is called *cheating*.

At the Academy, in flight school, and in the Marine Corps, we are trained to co-operate, to take many of our tests as a team. Even a Marine sniper has a spotter, someone to "call the shots."

One thing I loved about being a helicopter gunship pilot was that my "mechanic," aka "crew chief," flew with me. We flew as a five-man team, two pilots, two gunners, and one crew chief. We all depended upon each other.

I do not find that level of cooperation in the "corporate types" that I run into. The leadership style of most corporate executives can be summarized like this:

"I'm looking out for #1."

Or "Do as I tell you or I'll fire you."

Simply stated, military leaders lead via *mission* and corporate leaders lead via *money*.

When I meet entrepreneurs without military training, most lead by placing importance on "paychecks" and "stock options"—rather than on "mission." Their team will do what the leader wants done, as long as the paychecks keep coming.

If you ask anyone who has been in combat, they will tell you that as a situation becomes more hazardous, the teamwork gets stronger.

In most businesses, the opposite is true: Team work disintegrates when conditions become hazardous. When the going gets tough, civilians fix bayonets and often stab each other in the back.

What makes this book different from other books written for aspiring entrepreneurs is that it focuses on core strengths and leadership skills… because all entrepreneurs must be leaders.

The *New York Times* posted this quote by Pvt. Michael Armendariz-Clark, USMC on September 20, 2001, *"We signed up knowing the risk. Those innocent people in New York didn't go to work thinking there was any kind of risk."*

That quote can be applied to all entrepreneurs and anyone who wants to become an entrepreneur. It's obvious that there are risks entrepreneurs must take… and they're the same risks that employees *avoid*.

Different Leadership

While flying over a battlefield in Vietnam, I noticed something that startled me:

We were getting our butts kicked.

The South Vietnamese, our troops, were fleeing—not fighting. The Viet Cong and North Vietnamese troops were, literally, shooting them in the back.

Back on our aircraft carrier, during the debrief, I asked my commanding officer, "Why do their Vietnamese fight harder than our Vietnamese?" As you might guess, my question was not answered.

In the world of business, the same is often true. Many business leaders believe that leadership is simply telling people what to do, paying their employees more, or threatening to pay them less or fire them.

Other leaders, like Steve Jobs, have the power to create Apple fanatics, customers who swear undying loyalty and devotion to a brand to buying its products. Think of it this way: Apple does not have to sell its products. Loyal customers buy their products.

If you want to be a great entrepreneurial leader, it is important to know the differences between selling and buying, inspiration and motivation.

In my first squadron in Vietnam, my first CO inspired us to both fly and fight. Most of the young pilots loved him. We would die for him.

In another squadron, most of the same pilots despised the new CO. We did not trust him, nor did we believe a word he said. He used manipulation and intimidation to get us to do what he wanted done. I would not follow this leader to the latrine.

In the 1995 movie *Braveheart*, Mel Gibson plays William Wallace, a revolutionary in the Scottish people's fight for independence and there is a scene where Robert the Bruce, the future King of the Scots (played by Angus MacFayden) asks his father a question similar to the question I asked my commanding officer. Robert the Bruce wanted to know why William Wallace and his troops fought harder than his troops. He wanted to know why William Wallace's troops fought for free, had no food, no money, no shelter, and yet fought so fiercely. Robert the Bruce also said he had to force his troops to fight, threaten to take their land away, even to harm their wives and children, to get them to fight for him.

Robert the Bruce wanted to know exactly what I wanted to know when I asked, "Why do their Vietnamese fight harder than our Vietnamese?" I had thoughts of my own on why that might be the case...

There are those who lead via intimidation and leaders who lead by inspiration. Your job is to decide the type of leader you want to be.

Corporate Leadership vs. Military Leadership

Entering the corporate world in 1974 was quite a shock. I had been in a military environment for nine years, four at the Academy and five in the Marine Corps. It took me about a year to comprehend the difference between the two environments—corporate and military— and the differences in leadership styles.

Finally I began to recognize and understand the differences. In the military, leadership is internal. In the corporate world, leadership is external.

In the military, a culture of leadership begins when a new recruit enters boot camp, or a future officer enters officer candidate school or a service academy. The military culture is infused into each person, morning and night, whether an enlisted man or woman or an officer candidate. If the new recruit does not fit into the culture, they are washed out.

When the military promotes its new leaders, the new leaders come from within, not from the outside. They come from the ranks. In other words, the Marine Corps would never have a Commandant who was not a Marine.

In the civilian world, leadership often comes from the outside. A new employee is given a brief interview, shown to their desk, and expected to do the job.

When a new CEO is hired in the corporate world, they are often hired from the outside. Rarely have they been infused with the culture of the organization they are expected to lead. In many cases, the only thing the leaders and the employees have in common is that they all work for the same company.

Today, as an entrepreneur, running my own businesses, I focus on internal leadership. For example, because The Rich Dad Company is an education company, we have a company culture that respects education and learning. Every week, the entire company reads, studies, and discusses articles or subjects that keeps us in touch, up to date, and aware of financial events affecting our customers, our families, and our world.

Some of the subjects we study are real estate versus stocks, Keynesian economics, the gold standard versus paper money, taxes, and financial panics. Bottom line: The Rich Dad Company practices what it preaches and what it teaches to those we serve.

You have no idea how difficult this simple cultural event— making and taking time for everyone in The Rich Dad Company to be students—can be. We are, after all, an education company… and that is the culture that must be instilled and supported. A few previous leaders of our company (brought in, ironically, from the outside) would hold meetings, only to tell people what to do. There was no education, no learning, and very little two-way communication. It was leadership from the outside, not from the inside. Those leaders were asked to change, or leave.

Another example of the Rich Dad culture is that every employee is encouraged to be an entrepreneur and to start their own business. There is no fear of being fired for being a part-time entrepreneur. All employees are encouraged to ask our CEO and President, as well as Kim and me, for advice about building and growing their businesses. We have employees who are building real estate investment businesses, movie and documentary film businesses, and on-line marketing businesses. We put a high priority on practicing what we preach within our own company.

All of you who have served in the military know that the military branches are educational organizations. Everyone, from enlisted men and women to senior officers, are constantly learning. The military is a culture of education—from day one.

This is not true in the civilian business world. I remember being disgusted when I went to corporate "educational" events where people came to party or play golf, rather than learn.

To become a successful entrepreneur, I strongly suggest you take the military's culture of constant education and constant training to heart and instill that culture in your business. It may take awhile, since most civilians without military experience may have gone to school, but most have not worked in a culture of constant education and training.

If you can instill this culture inside your company, your company will be lead from the inside, by the people who actually make the business run, not executives who lead from the outside.

This book is written as a guide to prepare you to handle those risks. And there's good news for those who have served in the military: You already have the education and training, the core strengths, *the spiritual willpower*, and the *sense of mission* required to endure the rigors of being an entrepreneur. If you want guarantees of success, a steady paycheck, and benefits, it's probably best you keep your day job.

There is another reason I have written this book. I believe that the United States and the world face a massive problem, the problem of unemployment and underemployment.

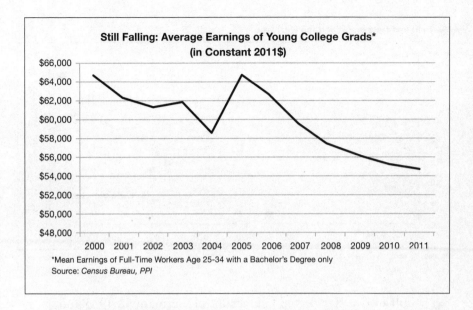

Today, with youth unemployment high, we have a global "lost generation," a generation of young people between the ages of 18 and 35 who are missing a critical window of real life experience, either unemployed or stuck in a job that does not challenge them. Odds are that many in this "lost generation" will struggle for the rest of their life.

Will History Repeat Itself?

Pictured on the following page is a chart from a very dark time in world history. It is a chart that illustrates the relationship between the rise in unemployment in Germany and the rise of the Nazi Party.

German unemployment and the Nazi vote

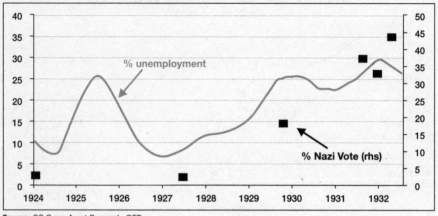

Source: *SG Cross Asset Research, GFD*

Adolf Hitler was elected Chancellor of Germany in 1933 and approximately 80 million people lost their lives. World War II, fought between 1939 and 1945, was an Industrial-Age War, fought by rich nations with industrial power.

Today's, terrorism is an Information-Age War, led by angry (and often poor) people, with access to low-cost, high-performance technology. Today a terrorist with charismatic leadership skills can create their own military force, using Facebook, Twitter, and Instagram. Today, cell phones can be more powerful than nuclear weapons. Today's Information-Age terrorism can spread rapidly and grow in ways that are virtually invisible.

Add these facts to this mix of data: In 1970, America had the highest rate of high school graduation in the world. Today, it has the lowest, ranking at 23 of 28 countries surveyed.

While a few high school dropouts do go on to lead great lives, a high proportion make up the long-term unemployed, the homeless, the welfare recipients and the incarcerated.

This is why I founded The Rich Dad Company and became an entrepreneur in financial education. It is tough becoming an entrepreneur without financial education, which is why I became an entrepreneur in education, *outside* the school system.

America Today

Now look at a chart on long-term unemployment in America today.

Today, we do not have an Adolf Hitler. Today we have the rise of terrorism, and anger fueled by rising food prices and rising youth unemployment.

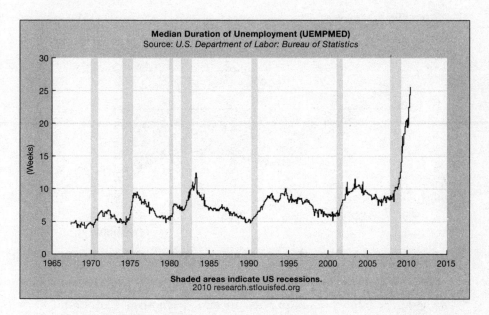

Median Duration of Unemployment (UEMPMED)
Source: *U.S. Department of Labor: Bureau of Statistics*

Shaded areas indicate US recessions.
2010 research.stlouisfed.org

The reason entrepreneurs are important is because only real entrepreneurs create real jobs and real prosperity.

Who's Killing Our Jobs?

While our veterans were serving our country our corporate leaders were busy "outsourcing jobs," sending jobs overseas.

Since pictures are worth thousands of words, I will let the following 'pictures' tell you the story of the freedom we defended.

Here's a sobering headline: Top U.S. Corporations Outsource More Than 2.4 Million Jobs Over Last Decade.

This graph tells the story:

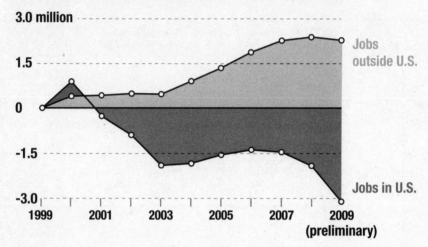

Where The Jobs Are Going

U.S.-based multinational companies added jobs overseas during the 2000s and cut them at home. Cumulative change since 1999

As you can see from the chart above, the economic recession has had little impact on corporate America's patriotism. Corporate America is hiring, but it's not hiring American workers.

In 2009, representatives of many of the nation's most powerful corporations attended the 2009 Strategic Outsourcing Conference to talk about how to send American jobs overseas. Conference organizers polled the more than 70 senior executives who attended the conference about the behavior of their companies in response to the recession. The majority said their companies increased outsourcing in response to the downturn, with only 9 percent saying they terminated some outsourcing agreements.

Here's a different chart that tells the same story:

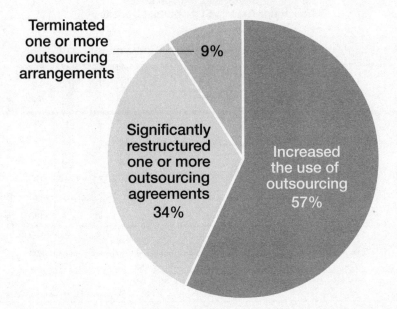

During the past year, in response to the economic downturn, our company has...

Terminated one or more outsourcing arrangements — 9%

Significantly restructured one or more outsourcing agreements 34%

Increased the use of outsourcing 57%

According to the research, the primary reason for outsourcing was to "reduce operating costs." According to the research, only a relatively small percent of respondents (just over 10 percent) said their reason for outsourcing was for "access to world-class capabilities." This means companies outsourced to save money, not to make better products.

Loss of Tax Revenue

The chart below illustrates the reason state governments are in the red. When jobs leave a state, tax revenues decrease.

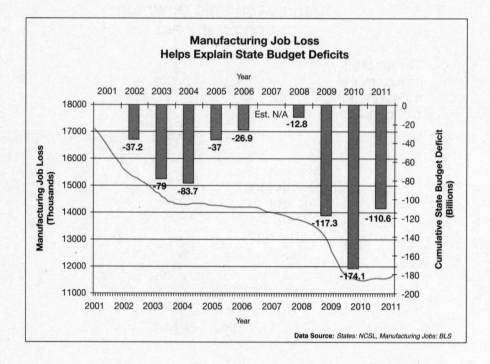

**Manufacturing Job Loss
Helps Explain State Budget Deficits**

Data Source: *States: NCSL, Manufacturing Jobs: BLS*

Unfortunately, for some of these companies, sending American jobs overseas isn't enough. They also want to bring the profits back into the United States with as little tax liability as possible. Cisco Systems, which had 26 percent of its workforce abroad at the start of the decade but 46 percent of its workforce abroad by the end, is currently involved in a lobbying campaign titled "Win America" calling for a tax repatriation holiday that would let big corporations "bring money they have stashed overseas back to the United States at a dramatically lower tax rate."

Asking for Your Service Again

As you can tell by these charts and graphs, your services are needed—this time at home. America is in trouble. America needs jobs. And the world needs entrepreneurs. Governments cannot create real jobs. America needs entrepreneurs because only real entrepreneurs can create real and sustainable jobs and real, lasting prosperity.

Simply put, when our government creates jobs our taxes increase. When taxes increase, life becomes more expensive, people suffer, our economy suffers, and our country grows weaker. When entrepreneurs create jobs, those jobs generate taxes, our debt goes down, we export, and our country grows stronger.

In this book I am asking our service men and women to serve once again, this time at home. And this time as entrepreneurs. I believe that the men and women of our armed services have the unique skills and training to be great entrepreneurs.

How the Military Trains Great Entrepreneurs

Education is a big word. Education is more than the 3 Rs, reading, 'riting, and 'rithmetic.

The problem with traditional education is that schools focus on teaching the brain. We are human beings, not human brains.

Pictured below is a diagram of education for the whole human being, a diagram of four different intelligences.

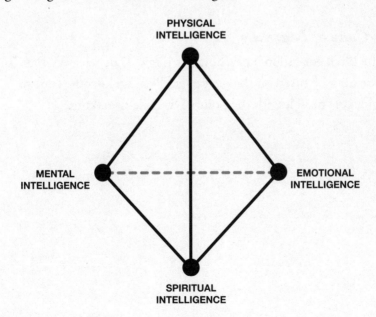

As we all know, all human beings are different. In one family alone, you can have four children—from the same parents—who are amazingly different. Even twins can be very different *beings*.

For *true education* to work, education must inspire all four intelligences. True *learning* requires that all four intelligences are engaged. For example, learning to play golf requires all four intelligences. Anyone who has played golf knows that the game of golf requires physical, mental, emotional, and spiritual intelligence.

The problem with traditional education is that our schools focus primarily on mental intelligence, with little attention paid to the other intelligences.

Physical Intelligence

The reason *physical intelligence* is at the top of this diagram is because *all learning is physical*. For example, for a child learning to walk, the learning process relies on physical intelligence, more than mental intelligence. In school, learning to read, write, and do arithmetic is primarily a physical process. Like learning to walk, the student needs to *do* something.

The Cone of Learning

In 1969, educational psychologist Edgar Dale released The Cone of Learning pictured on the next page. Please take some time to familiarize yourself with the points Dr. Dale is making.

Cone of Learning

After 2 weeks we tend to remember		Nature of Involvement
90% of what we say and do	Doing the Real Thing	Active
	Simulating the Real Experience	
	Doing a Dramatic Presentation	
70% of what we say	Giving a Talk	
	Participating in a Discussion	
50% of what we hear and see	Seeing it Done on Location	Passive
	Watching a Demonstration	
	Looking at an Exhibit Watching a Demonstration	
	Watching a Movie	
30% of what we see	Looking at Pictures	
20% of what we hear	Hearing Words (Lecture)	
10% of what we read	Reading	

Source: Cone of Learning adapted from Dale, (1969)

As you can see—at the bottom of the Cone of Learning—reading and writing (the staples of most schools) are the least effective ways for a student to retain what they're taught.

At the top of the Cone, simulations and doing the real thing are the most effective way to learn. In other words, you learn more by doing. Making the point another way: It is almost impossible to learn to walk or play golf by simply reading a book or listening to a lecture.

Making matters worse, our schools punish students for making mistakes. That would be like punishing a baby for falling down or a golfer for making a bad shot. If a student does not make mistakes, the learning is retarded.

Physical intelligence is located in the body, and it's also called *muscle memory*. For example, a person learning to play golf, will repeat, repeat, and repeat different shots, making mistake after mistake, until the muscles remember the proper physical process.

The second highest level of learning, according to the Cone of Learning, is called *simulation*. In sports it is called *practice*, in the arts it is called *rehearsal*, and in science it is called *experiments*.

For those of you who have been in the military, you understand the importance of *simulation*. It's how the military teaches and trains. For example, while in flight school at Pensacola, student pilots spent nearly as much time *practicing crashing* as they did *flying*. After receiving my wings, I was stationed at Camp Pendleton, California, for advanced guns and rockets training in preparation for Vietnam. Again, on every training flight, we practiced crashing, equipment failure, and other emergencies. I am alive today because I learned how to fly a helicopter with—or without—an engine. I could never have learned to fly by listening to lectures, reading a book, and being afraid of crashing. I needed the hours I spent in the simulator.

Great athletes are gifted with physical intelligence. Yet even gifted athletes must "practice, practice, practice," making mistake after mistake, until their physical genius emerges.

I like to look at the word genius as the geni-in-us or the magician in us. When a professional athlete's genius appears, creating magic on the playing field, success and (very often) big money pours into his or her life.

In traditional education, when a child makes mistakes the child is punished. Hence many students leave school—having memorized all the "right" answers and living in terror of making mistakes—but unable to really do much. They learned to avoid making mistakes rather than practicing 'mistakes' and learning from them.

In traditional education, a student who makes too many mistakes is labeled *slow* or *stupid*—yet in real life—a person who makes the most mistakes and learns from their mistakes is often called *successful*.

The reason I believe many military personnel have the potential to become great entrepreneurs is because, in the military—regardless of branch of service—each person is tested to the breaking point, physically, emotionally, spiritually, and mentally. Anyone who has gone through 'recruit training' knows the military first breaks you down then builds you up in all four intelligences, rebuilding a stronger human being.

Many civilians go through life, avoiding being 'broken down' which I believe is why many civilians may be smart intellectually, academic "A" students or technical *whiz kids*, but weak in one or more of the other intelligences.

When a recruit *washes out*, most do not just fail mentally. They fail in several, if not all four, intelligences. As John F. Kennedy, President and World War II war hero, said:

> "*A young man who does not have what it takes to perform military service is not likely to have what it takes to make a living. Today's military rejects include tomorrow's hard-core unemployed.*"

Unemployment Statistics

After the real estate and stock market crash of 2007, unemployment (including unemployment among our youth) hit all-time highs.

The following chart shows U.S. unemployment rates. You will notice that there are differences between the official government statistics and the *Shadowstats.*

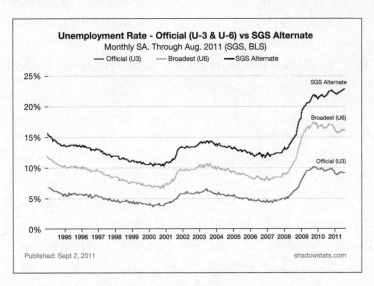

What Will You Choose to Believe?

There are many reasons why unemployment is high. One reason is that jobs are moving overseas to lower-wage countries. Another reason is that technology is replacing workers, much like the car replaced the horse. Today, we must require our workers to be retrained, reeducated, and transitioned into the world of technology. Simply put, the choices today are: High-tech jobs, low-wage jobs, or long-term unemployment. It's not surprising that we continue to see the middle class shrink.

The primary reasons I am not an "unemployed baby boomer" today is because, when I left the Marine Corps in 1974, I chose to learn to become an entrepreneur, rather than go back to school, get my MBA, and become an employee... a corporate executive. If I had become an employee, as my poor dad encouraged me to be, I am certain I would be one of those executives who would have lost their job to "outsourcing" or to a younger, tech-savvy worker who was willing to work for less.

The good news was that I had four years of education at a military academy and five years as a pilot in the U.S. Marine Corps. That means I had a well-rounded education—the physical, mental, emotional, and spiritual training required to become an entrepreneur. I still had a lot to learn, and I continue to study and learn today. But my military education and training prepared me for the tests required to become an entrepreneur.

The following are my ideas on how military education and training prepared me for life as an entrepreneur.

Mental Intelligence

Mental intelligence takes place in the brain. It is still a physical learning process. For example, learning to read is a physical process. When learning to speak a new language, the person repeats, repeats, and repeats until the brain remembers the words.

People who are gifted with mental intelligence often become teachers, scholars, and attorneys.

Mental intelligence, in my opinion, is the least important of the four intelligences for success as an entrepreneur. A true entrepreneur, like a true leader, does not have to be smartest person on the team. That means a true entrepreneur must be a leader, smart enough to lead smarter and better-educated people into the battlefield of business.

True leadership does require the next intelligence.

Emotional Intelligence

Emotional intelligence is our ability to control our emotions.

We have all lost our tempers. When we lose our tempers, we demonstrate low emotional intelligence. An emotionally intelligent person will experience anger, but not so much anger that it may cause them to do or say something stupid. They remain in control.

A person who cannot control their temper, or complains all the time, or is chronically depressed, is a person who demonstrates low emotional intelligence.

Examples of high emotional intelligence are when someone walks away rather than throws a punch, listens rather than argues, sees another person's point of view rather than defending their own, and does a great job without expecting praise.

Delayed gratification is also another indication of emotional intelligence. For example, a person who buys something they cannot afford—just because they want it now—is a person who cannot delay gratification. This is a sign of low emotional intelligence.

Military training does an outstanding job developing a person's emotional intelligence. How else can a person stay cool under fire, advance in the face of death, and persevere when others quit?

Most people remain employees rather than develop into entrepreneurs because they cannot control the emotion known as fear. Anyone who has served in the military knows that military training and service does not eliminate fear. The military trains you to think and operate in spite of your fear. It is the same ability required of entrepreneurs as they take on the challenges of launching and growing a business.

Emotional intelligence is located in the stomach. This is why people will say "I have a bad feeling in my gut" about something or someone. And this may be why ulcers, caused by fear and worry, are found in the stomach or intestines.

In my opinion, people with low emotional intelligence should not become entrepreneurs. Saying this in a more positive way: Becoming a successful entrepreneur requires the on-going development of your emotional intelligence.

The true leaders, in any field, have high emotional IQs.

Spiritual Intelligence

Spiritual intelligence is located in the heart. That is why the word courage comes from the French word, *le coeur*, which means the heart.

Greatness comes from the heart. So does death, which is why people die of heart attacks or from the devastation of a broken heart.

Again, the military does an outstanding job developing the spiritual intelligence of new recruits. People with high spiritual intelligence operate with a sense of mission, putting the mission and the team ahead of their own life.

As General Douglas McArthur said:

> *"It is fatal to enter a war without the will to win it."*

Training Entrepreneurs

To develop as an entrepreneur requires:

1. **Spiritual Intelligence**
   Spiritual intelligence is the most important of intelligences for entrepreneurs. Entrepreneurs require a strong sense of mission, a commitment to a higher purpose in life, a reason for going into business, apart from simply a desire to "make money."

   My first day at the Academy, my first job was to memorize the mission of the Academy. We were taught "mission is spiritual" and that spiritual power, spiritual intelligence, is what would get us through four years of hell.

As General George Patton once said:

"Live for something… rather than die for nothing."

2. Emotional Intelligence

Emotional intelligence is the second most important intelligence for entrepreneurs. Entrepreneurs must know how to remain cool under pressure, to think rather than react, and to know when to wait and when to strike.

Another quote from General Douglas McArthur that seems appropriate:

"Whoever said the pen is mightier than the sword obviously never encountered automatic weapons."

3. Physical Intelligence

Physical intelligence is the third most important intelligence for entrepreneurs. A person must have "know how." In the world of entrepreneurship, you achieve success and all that comes with it… only if you know what you're doing, and do what you promise to do.

As Winston Churchill said:

"We sleep safely at night because rough men stand ready to visit violence on those who would harm us."

4. Mental Intelligence

Mental intelligence is important, but it is the least important intelligence in the world of entrepreneurs.

Robert A. Heinlein, a civilian military contractor, summed it up this way:

"Civilians are like beans; you buy 'em as needed for any job which merely requires skill and savvy. But you can't buy fighting spirit."

This may be the basis for why some of the greatest and richest entrepreneurs never finished school. Being a great entrepreneur or serving your country requires all four intelligences, especially spiritual intelligence, the power to keep going when everything else is gone.

A classmate of mine from elementary school, Richie Richardson, was an Army LRRP, Long Range Reconnaissance Patrol, and spent as much time in Laos as in Vietnam. He once said to me: "I am alive today because dead men kept fighting."

Being an entrepreneur requires the same spirit.

A few entrepreneurs with strong spirits, but who never finished school are:

Steve Jobs: *Apple Computers*

Bill Gates: *Microsoft*

Henry Ford: *Ford Motor Company*

Walt Disney: *Disney Productions, Disneyland, Disney World*

Oprah Winfrey: *Oprah Winfrey Network*

Mark Zuckerberg: *Facebook*

Richard Branson: *Virgin Group*

Michael Dell: *Dell Computers*

Thomas Edison: *General Electric*

A good college education is essential for people who want to be doctors, lawyers, or executives, but it is not essential for people who want to be entrepreneurs.

You may be familiar with this saying: "Education is the door to the middle class."

My rich dad said, "Entrepreneurship is the elevator for the rich."

Mission, Courage, Sacrifice

In August of 1972, I was flying off LPH-3, the helicopter carrier USS Okinawa off the coast of Vietnam. My door gunner, a young corporal, had just received word that his wife had given birth to their first child, a son.

As the new father finished inspecting his M-60 door gun, I tapped him on the shoulder. I wanted to be sure he was OK with flying that day. I asked him, "Is it OK with you if your son grows up without a father?"

Understanding my concern, the young Marine smiled and said; "Yes, sir. It's OK with me. I'm ready to go." He then smiled again, assuring me he really was "ready to go"—ready to die if necessary. Then he said: "Lieutenant, you do your job and I'll do mine."

Five months later, the young father returned home to meet his son for the first time. He had done his job and I had done mine.

As General George Patton said:

> *"The object of war is not to die for your country*
> *but to make the other bastard die for his."*

Two Years Later...

In June of 1974, my contract with the Marine Corps was fulfilled. I had been in the military for nine years, four years at a military academy and five years in the Marine Corps. In many ways, I had grown up in the military.

I drove off the Marine Corps Air Station at Kaneohe Bay, Hawaii and went to work for the Xerox Corporation in downtown Honolulu. It took awhile to adjust to the change in cultures.

It was not easy learning to work with civilians. It was not easy working with and associating with former "hippies," and people who spit on us and called us "baby-killers."

It wasn't easy working for a boss, a young guy who was close to my age but who had used his "student deferment" to avoid the draft, the war, and serving his country. It took a lot of emotional intelligence to bite my tongue every time he laughed and bragged about how he used his "student deferment" to avoid the draft and climb the corporate ladder while others were fighting and risking their lives in Vietnam.

In downtown Honolulu, the words used amongst "civilians" and the "corporate warriors" reflected a lack of emotional intelligence. When many of the corporate-class speak their words consistently reflect one emotion: fear. They repeatedly speak of "job security," worry about "being fired," obsess over "needing my paycheck" and "climbing the corporate ladder." I suspect they continue to ask themselves, "Can I afford to retire?"

In the corporate world, I was shocked to hear people repeatedly saying, "I can't." And "I might." They used words like "I'll try" and "I might" or "I hope". Those words are forbidden in the Marine Corps.

For those of you who have read my other books, you already know my rich dad would not allow his son and me to use those words. He often said, "Poor people say 'I can't afford' it more than rich people. Rich people ask, "How can I afford it?"

In the military, there are service personnel who speak the same fear-based words. They are called *lifers*, and they are seldom leaders. They are in the military to put in their "20" and retire.

In the military, the words leaders speak are spiritual words, coming from the heart and originating in their souls. Military education begins by teaching everyone to speak spiritual words, words like mission, courage, duty, honor, service, and code.

People who speak words that come from their souls inspire their spirit and become great warriors, entrepreneurs, and leaders in all walks of life.

Your Country Needs You

This book is written to speak to the warrior spirit in you. Once again, you are called on to serve your country, but this time not as a soldier but as an entrepreneur, a leader in the world of business.

I realize that many Americans despise the military. They have that right, guaranteed by our Constitution and the Bill of Rights. The right to speak freely is one the freedoms men and women in the military protect.

The U.S. military does not fight for the Republicans or the Democrats, for liberals or conservatives. The military serves and is willing to fight to protect the principles and freedoms of this great nation.

Freedom Is a Big Word

Freedom is a very, very big word. Most people have no idea how huge that word really is. There is freedom of religion and freedom of speech… and the U.S. military defends those freedoms.

In other countries, military forces fought to prevent the freedom of religion. We've seen religious freedom as the catalyst for unrest in all parts of the world, from the Middle East to Northern Ireland.

American service men and women fight for the freedom to worship or not worship, the right to believe in god or not believe in god, and the right to marry or not marry someone of a different religion. In my opinion, this is a freedom, a human right, worth fighting for.

Political Freedom

In Communist countries, there is only one official political party. Their military fights to defend the one-party system. In some countries, if you start your own political party, you will be locked away forever, or murdered by the military.

The American military will fight to defend our right to form political parties and to vote or not vote. In my opinion, that is another freedom, another right, worth fighting for.

As General William Westmoreland said:

> *"The military don't start wars. Politicians start wars."*

Freedom of Speech

In China, stand up comedians must submit their jokes to the government for approval before they can use them to make people laugh. In many countries, *The Daily Show* with Jon Stewart would not be allowed on the air.

In 1973, I landed at Norton Air Force Base in San Bernardino, California. My troops and I had just returned from our tour in Vietnam.

Outside the gates of the base were anti-war protestors. I could sense the fear and anger in the eyes of my men. One said, "Why do we fight for these people?"

Before allowing the Marines to face the abuse, to run the gauntlet, I asked the Marines to line up for my farewell address. "We did not fight for 'these people,'" I said, "we fight all people." "We fight for the freedom for all people to say what they want to say, even if you and I do not like what they say." That is the essence of freedom.

Pausing for a moment, allowing what I had just said to sink in, I then asked, "Do you understand what we fight for? Do you understand what many of our friends died for? Do you understand we fight for freedom and rights of all people, not for select groups of people."

After a quiet "Yes, sir," I thanked the young Marines for their service and that I was proud to have served with them. In silence, they shouldered their bags, turned, and walked through the protestors, with their heads held high, their backs straight, their eyes focused… saying nothing as spit, eggs, and verbal abuse were hurled at them.

Financial Freedom

When people see the chart on the next page, the one you saw at the start of this chapter, many become upset.

Where The Jobs Are Going

U.S.-based multinational companies added jobs overseas during the 2000s and cut them at home. Cumulative change since 1999

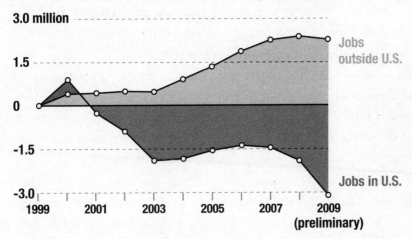

A few people say, "How can the government allow companies to do this?"

Again, the answer is: This is a right, a freedom, granted by our Constitution and the Bill of Rights. It is a freedom the U.S. military defends and protects. A business can hire or fire anyone in any country. In layman's terms, it's called free enterprise. In some circles, free enterprise is known as capitalism… a 'dirty word' to some. I suspect many of the same people who detest the U.S. military also detest the word capitalism. That may be because capitalism is not possible without a strong military. Without a strong military, our economy would be run by war lords, similar to those factions that run countries where the military is weak or corrupt.

The idea of free enterprise began in 1700 in America, and it led to the Boston Tea Party, the American Revolution, the Constitution, and the Bill of Rights. Americans were sick and tired of England's monarchy telling them how to do business and taxing them without representation in government.

The concept of free enterprise is the foundation for the American Dream. Many immigrants came to America from countries where your socio-economic status was determined by birth. If you were born into royalty, you were forever royalty; if you were born a peasant, you died a peasant.

The American Dream meant a person could come to America and, possibly, become American 'royalty.' Many people have achieved that dream and the U.S. military protects the right to that opportunity.

Capitalism is an economic system that allows businesses to be privately owned. This system aims for limited restrictions on trade and minimal government intervention. This means that a privately owned business can do business and hire (or fire) employees anywhere in the world. It shouldn't be surprising that labor unions and most employees do not agree with this freedom or right.

It is for these freedoms and rights the American military fights for and defends. In America, you are free to be a capitalist, a communist, or socialist… rich, poor, or middle class… Christian, Muslim, Jew, or atheist. It is for these freedoms we in the U.S. military are willing to give our lives.

Why I Wrote This Book

This book is written to ask for your service once again. America needs your help.

The following poem best summarizes my reason for writing this book:

It is the Soldier, not the minister
Who has given us freedom of religion.
It is the Soldier, not the reporter
Who has given us freedom of the press.
It is the Soldier, not the poet
Who has given us freedom of speech.
It is the Soldier, not the campus organizer
Who has given us freedom to protest.
It is the Soldier, not the lawyer
Who has given us the right to a fair trial.
It is the Soldier, not the politician

Who has given us the right to vote.
It is the Soldier who salutes the flag,
Who serves beneath the flag,
And whose coffin is draped by the flag,
Who allows the protester to burn the flag.

And—I will add—it is the solider who is now called upon to become an entrepreneur because only real entrepreneurs can create real jobs and real prosperity.

As General Douglas McArthur warned:

*"I am concerned for the security of our great Nation;
not so much because of any treat from without,
but because of the insidious forces working from within."*

You may recall the words in the Oath of Enlightenment at the beginning of this book:

*I do solemnly swear that I support and defend the
Constitution of the United States against all enemies,
foreign and domestic...*

This is why this book was written and dedicated to the men and women of our armed forces—and why I ask you to consider becoming an entrepreneur, in service to our country.

In the next chapter I will go into what it takes to become an entrepreneur. And I will tell you this: You already have the basic training and instincts to be a great one.

Chapter Two

HOW TO BECOME AN ENTREPRENEUR

It's been said that entrepreneurship isn't for everyone. That's one side of the coin. Here's another.

I'm often asked, "Can anyone become an entrepreneur?"

And my answer is always the same: Yes. A person who cleans houses is an entrepreneur. A medical doctor in private practice is an entrepreneur. So was Steve Jobs, founder of Apple.

Entrepreneurs come in all shapes and sizes. Most entrepreneurial businesses are small, only one person or 'mom and pop' (often husband and wife) operations. A few people build mega-businesses and change the world.

The question that always follows is the logical follow-up… but the answer isn't quite so cut and dried. You probably guessed it: How do I get started?

There is a lot to learn so I always recommend studying, investigating, and doing as much market research as possible before starting a business. Your local SBA (Small Business Administration) office can be a wealth of information. So, of course, is the Internet.

Once you decide on the business or type of business you want to go into, I suggest going to work for someone who is already in that business. For example, if you want to start a restaurant, get a job in a restaurant, working to learn. Learning ever facet of the business. When you work to learn you gain something much more important than money, you gain wisdom, experience, and a creative edge.

The best business school for entrepreneurs is McDonald's. In my opinion, McDonald's has the best business systems in the world. That's why they are a global organization. I would work at McDonald's, learning every position—from cashier to cook to shift manager.

The pay may not be great, but the education and experience is priceless. Think of McDonald's as a great business school for entrepreneurs.

I got my first business experience working to learn when I worked for my rich dad for free. In return, he paid me by teaching me business lessons most people will never learn. College professors or PhDs, like my poor dad, my real father, may be well-educated but lack on-the-job training and in-the-trenches experience.

Working at McDonald's or with a good network marketing company will give you real-life business experience. Always remember this: It's not what you know that makes you rich, but what you don't know that makes you poor. Experience is priceless. And it can also be expensive.

Most entrepreneurs fail due to lack of experience, not a lack of money. If you have experience, you can always create more money. Being an entrepreneur is like being a platoon, trapped behind enemy lines, living off the land and the enemy. As an unknown Marine 2dLt in Vietnam said:

"Courage is endurance for one moment more…"

I believe that same courage applies to entrepreneurs.

What are some of the skills entrepreneurs must have? The number one skill is the ability to sell. Why? Because… Sales = Income.

That is why Donald Trump and I recommend network marketing as a way to increase your sales and leadership skills.

The number one reason why entrepreneurs fail is that they are terrified of rejection. Their fear paralyses them. And then—if they overcome their fear—they lack the communication skills to make a presentation and ask for the money they need to launch the business.

In the military it's known as giving orders and receiving orders. Every time an order is given, it is a sales job. If your troops do not respect you, they will not follow your orders.

So, how did you learn these skills?

It takes practice. At the Academy, we are taught to give orders to our peers. You have no idea how hard it is to get 18-year-old boys to follow orders.

When I left the Marine Corps, I went to work for Xerox, in downtown Honolulu. That decision was less about the money I would make, my paycheck, but for the sales education and real-world experience. For two years I was on the short list to be fired.

When I asked my rich dad how I could become a better salesman, he answered my question with a question. "How many sales calls do you make a day?" he asked.

My reply was: "On a good day, five presentations; on a bad day, none."

Without hesitation he said, "Your problem is your failure rate is too slow. If you want to learn to sell, fail faster."

Fail faster. Okay.

Later that week, I went to a non-profit organization and volunteered to "dial-for-dollars" in the evenings, asking for donations. My goal was to make 30 contacts each evening... so I could fail faster.

About two months later, my sales stats at Xerox started to go up. And during my last two years with Xerox I was either number one or number two in sales. When my sales went up, my income went up.

The same principle of "fail faster" is taught in the military. While at Camp Pendleton in California, preparing for Vietnam, my flight instructor had me "crashing" my aircraft everytime we flew. He wanted to make sure I was an expert at auto-rotations.

In 1972, 27 miles off the coast of Vietnam, the engine on the Huey I was flying quit and we dove into the South China Sea. Pictured on the back cover of this book is 1Lt Ted Greene and me walking across a flight line. He and I were the pilots in charge of our team. All five on our aircraft came back, simply because we practiced "crashing" on every training flight. But more than crashing, we practiced crashing as a team. When our engine quit and we all knew what to do. Our crew of five swam for over five hours, 27 miles off the coast of Vietnam, before finally being rescued. The team got stronger as ocean conditions worsened and exhaustion set in.

I rarely see that happening in the business world. When times get tough, most employees ask for a pay raise or go looking for a new job.

On the front cover of this book is a photo of 1Lt Joe Ezell and me. He and I crashed onto the back of a Navy ship, due to a dual hydraulics failure. As far as we know, we are the only Huey pilots to that have survived a dual-hydraulics failure. Simply put, without hydraulics, the Huey does not fly. And without hours of coordinated practice, as a crew, we would be dead today.

The same discipline related to education and practice applies in business. Too many new entrepreneurs jump into business without experience, invest their life savings, and are soon broke. That's why I often say, it's not a lack of money that causes a business to go bust, it's a lack of real world experience. And how does a person gain real-world business experience? By falling down and standing back up… again and again. It's called entrepreneurial spirit.

The good news is that today's high-tech world and the Internet allows entrepreneurs to experiment faster and make mistakes with less risk in sales and marketing campaigns. The counterpoint to that is there is much more competition today, as compared to when I started out in business.

Rich Dad Advisor and good friend Blair Singer is one of the best sales trainers in the world. Major companies like Singapore Airlines, L'Oréal, HSBC, IBM, CitiGroup, and United Healthcare bring him in to teach their teams to sell.

Blair has written a book titled *SalesDogs*, which presents an interesting and effective way for you to find your unique selling style. Blair's company also offers on-line sales development programs. He is a great teacher.

The Power of Mentors

A great way to use and leverage the experience and education of success entrepreneurs Is to find a mentor. A mentor is someone who has already gone where you want to go. Someone who has already faced the challenges you're likely to face and who has found solutions that work.

In Vietnam we used locals and Vietnamese Marines for local knowledge. I do the same thing in business.

And while writing a Business Plan is an important step in the process of launching a business, I always suggest that entrepreneurs write an Education Plan as well. When you write your Business Plan, you'll discover many things you need to learn, so creating an "Education Plan" will guide your entrepreneurial development program. Rich Dad Advisor Garrett Sutton has written a book on writing business plans, *Writing Winning Business Plans*. It's a great guide and will save you a lot of time.

There are many organizations, such as EO (Entrepreneurs' Organization), which has chapters all over the world. It is an organization committed to training, educating, and mentoring entrepreneurs.

The Law of Compensation

This law, the Law of Compensation, is important for anyone who wants to be financially successful in life. The Law of Compensation states, "Your income goes up as your education, experience, and wisdom goes up."

For example, let's say I want to be a professional golfer and win The Masters golf tournament. That means I'd better start practicing, studying, playing, and competing as soon as possible. Although it may cost me more money than I earn for many years, if I stick with my practice, study, playing, and competing, my income and success will increase over the years. If you win The Masters, the doors of golf heaven open.

The Law of Compensation applies to entrepreneurs. For years, Steve Jobs and Steve Wozniak worked in a garage, building crude "hobby" computers. Today, Apple products are known for their innovation and sleek lines and have changed the way the world communicates. The founders became billionaires working from a garage.

I'm sure you've heard all the abyssmal statistics on the number of businesses—the vast majority—that fail. As you might expect, I like to look at the other side of the coin related to those stats.

I believe that failure is the path to success. One reason why many smart people, people who did well in school, are not rich is because they were taught in school that making mistakes means you are (or makes you) stupid. In reality, making mistakes makes you smarter, if you learn from your mistakes.

As General Colin Powell has stated:

"There are no secrets to success. It is the result of preparation, hard work, and learning from failure."

In the military, we spend most of our time studying and practicing, rather than fighting. That is why the U.S. military is powerful, effective, and deadly. Do the same in business, and your chances of success will improve significantly.

Remember, Henry Ford went bankrupt five times before the Ford Motor Company was born. Thomas Edison failed over 1,000 times before inventing the electric light bulb and birth of General Electric.

In business, the courage to fail until you succeed is known as the Spirit of Entrepreneurship.

Every person who has served in the U.S. military has the same DNA of education, training, learning, discipline, and courage in their souls.

To this day, I don't understand why traditional education punishes students for making mistakes. I guess the goal of traditional schools is to train people to be employees, not entrepreneurs. In traditional business, if you're an employee and you make too many mistakes there's a good chance you'll be fired.

Entrepreneurs who make the most mistakes and learn from their mistakes, get rich. That is why entrepreneurs must be leaders.

In business, most employees with advanced degrees such as MBAs are not leaders. They are managers. They manage one aspect of the business process, such as marketing or accounting or legal. These processes, all of them, are important and essential for a business to grow and be profitable.

The problem with being an entrepreneur is that your job is to create these business processes, not manage them. Once the processes are developed, then you hire managers, often called executives. Once you have managers running your business, you can move on and start your next business or strategize and plan ways to grow or globalize your business. But this can only happen if you have good business processes and strong managers in place.

Again, I believe this illustrates why writing an Education Plan—as well as a Business Plan—is important. Entrepreneurs must be learning constantly—about the big picture of a business, about innovation, about global opportunities and markets Entrepreneurs are generalists. Managers or executives are specialists, focused on only one process of a business, such as marketing or accounting. An entrepreneur must know a little about marketing, systems and accounting, then hire executives who are experts in those fields as well as every other critical process within a business.

In my business, my team gets together twice a year as part of the Code of Honor in our Education Plan. We learn and study together. This team is my team of Rich Dad Advisors. All have written books for the Rich Dad Advisor series and we operate by a Code of Honor.

I have a team of advisors because I am not the smartest person on my team. I do not need to be... if I have a smart team of specialists who are at the top of their game.

In simple terms, true entrepreneurs are generalists related to all business processes. A generalist knows a little about a lot of things. Executives are specialists, experts in only one area or business process. A specialist knows a lot about a little.

This is why working for McDonald's is a great place to learn to a generalist, with an overview of many business processes. Working for McDonald's is different and better than working for Walmart, because most McDonald's stores are small, compact, and precise, while Walmart stores are vast.

I can hear the cries of outrage already! "Are you saying I must work for McDonald's if I want to be an entrepreneur?"

No. What I am saying is that you must be an active, aggressive learner.

For example, in high school I was a screw off. I got by with Cs and a even a few Fs. But when machine guns and rockets were strapped to my helicopter, at Camp Pendleton, I knew my next stop was Vietnam. Suddenly I became an extremely active and focused learner.

If you're going to be an entrepreneur, I suggest you cultivate the same interest in learning. If you believe you know all the answers, you will probably say good-bye to your money, your family's money, and your investor's money. I know because I have lost a lot of money in the process of getting my real-life entrepreneurial education. To repeat my statement from earlier in this chapter: Successful entrepreneurship is not about what you know... but what you don't know.

I'm often asked what an Education Plan should include. The answer to that question is that the list is endless. A few basics you'll want to include are taxes, debt financing, marketing, technology, sales, accounting, law, and human resources.

You don't have to go back to school but you do have to be an active and continuous learner, just as you are (or were) in the military. Military leaders know that the enemy and theaters of operation are always changing, always improving. That is why education is vital to a strong military.

In business, you can read books or take weekend courses. Most important of all: You must be an active, aggressive, ambitious learner or you will be out of business before you know it. Being an entrepreneur requires far more study than being an employee.

For example, let's take a look at taxes. Pictured on the next page is the CASHFLOW Quadrant, introduced in an early Rich Dad book by the same name.

In the world of business there are four different and distinct groups of people.

They are:

Es = employees

Ss = the self-employed, small business owners, or specialists

Bs = big business owners with 500 employees or more

Is = professional investors

Our schools train most students to become employees in the E quadrant or specialists, such as doctors or lawyers, in the S quadrant.

Taxes are different for each group.

It takes a lot of financial intelligence to pay less and less taxes, legally.

It seems hard to believe that what made America great and what is still the essence of the American Dream—the small business entrepreneurs—pay the highest taxes?

But it's true. That is why study, especially the study of taxes and tax strategies, is vital for entrepreneurs. I meet many successful entrepreneurs, who make a lot of money, but always complain about paying high taxes. They pay the highest taxes because they do not study and understand taxes and how to put the government's incentives, aka the Tax Code, to work for them. Many successful entrepreneurs who don't take the time to study taxes and find a great tax specialist, focus on making more money—instead of keeping more of the money they make. In my opinion that's not very smart.

Information-Age Oxymoron

Is it fair, the varying tax percentages that those in the different quadrants pay?

Probably not. But no one ever said that life is fair. And it's based in what our military fights for: freedom to choose life as an employee, an entrepreneur, or an investor. If we fought for everything to be fair we would have to become a socialist or communist society. I'll say it again: The U.S. military fights for our rights, the right to be capitalists, socialists, or communists.

Most people choose job security and accept the fact that they'll pay relatively high taxes in the E quadrant. Yet in today's world job security has become an oxymoron. Most jobs in today's global marketplace are not secure as low-wage countries vie for production and service contracts and jobs.

There was some degree of job security for the World War II generation. For that generation, a person got a job, worked at the job for years before retiring and living happily ever after.

Beginning with the Vietnam-era generation, there was less and less job security. It's said that most young people today will have five to seven careers, which means they may have to be re-trained before being re-hired.

For the World War II generation, age and seniority were assets. The longer a person worked for a company, the more valuable they became. The more value they contributed, the more money they were paid. For the most part, those days are long gone.

In today's workplace, age and seniority are liabilities. Most businesses today are looking for tech-savvy young people who will work for less than their older counterparts. I have a number of friends, graduates from great schools such as Harvard and Stanford, who were "let go" at age 50. They are too old, too expensive, obsolete, and could be (in some cases) replaced by a computer program.

Today the concept of job security is an idea for people living in the past.

Another sobering picture is what lies ahead for Social Security for the baby-boom generation.

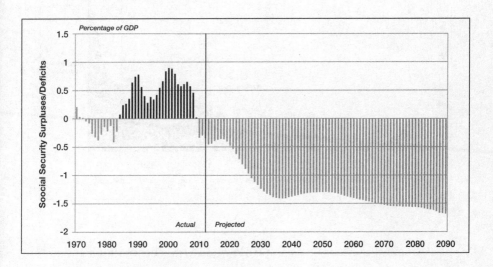

It's hard to look at charts like these without having a dozen questions swirl around in your brain. Does this mean Social Security is toast? What does this means for those who are counting on Social Security to cover the cost of their retirement? Can we continue to count on the government to take care of our parents and the millions of retirees... and me and my family when I retire?

It's these questions, and ones like them, that have people worried and fearful about the future. Entrepreneurs know that they can create the future—income, jobs, opportunities that will let them take personal responsibility for their financial futures.

The following chart shows the national debt of the United States.

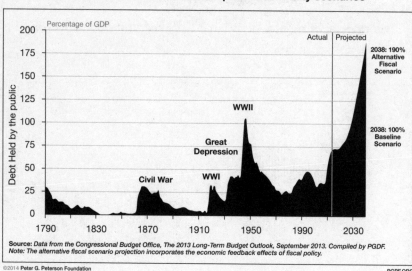

U.S. debt is on an unsustainable path under many scenarios

Source: Data from the Congressional Budget Office, The 2013 Long-Term Budget Outlook, September 2013. Compiled by PGDF.
Note: The alternative fiscal scenario projection incorporates the economic feedback effects of fiscal policy.

©2014 Peter G. Peterson Foundation   PGPF.ORG

Consider these projects at a time when U.S. corporations are outsourcing more and more jobs overseas.

So if job security has become an oxymoron, what's the solution?

I recommend stepping back and taking a look at the big picture. For example, the words job security originate from the emotion fear, the fear of losing your job.

As I've stated in the previous chapter, the military does a great job training young recruits to control their emotions, which increases their emotional intelligence.

People who live in fear of losing their job are people with low emotional intelligence. They may be well educated, very smart, good, honest, hard working people, but when your emotions run your life, your emotional IQ goes down.

Many entrepreneurs become entrepreneurs because they want their independence, their 'financial freedom.' The word freedom is rooted in a person's spiritual intelligence.

I believe that one reason the Viet Cong fought harder than we did was because they were spiritually motivated. They wanted to win more than we did. They were tired of "foreigners" from the China, France, then the United States, telling them what to do. It was no different than the early American revolutionaries, under George Washington, fighting to get the English out of America. As General George Marshall said:

"Military power wins battles… but spiritual power wins wars."

The same is true in entrepreneurship.

In many ways, the path to entrepreneurship is a spiritual one. The United States and much of the world is in trouble—financially, morally, and spiritually. The United States and the world economy needs you, because you have been trained mentally, physically, emotionally and spiritually.

We are in trouble because many of our leaders lack this multi-dimensional education and development. Many of our leaders remind me of one of my bosses at Xerox, the boss who was proud that he used his student deferment to avoid the draft and serving his country. He knew he could serve his country without going to Vietnam, but he simply did not want to be of service. He only wanted to make money and climb the corporate ladder. The world is filled with people like this, and many are in positions of influence and leadership.

So I write this book and ask you to do some soul searching, much like the soul searching I had to do when I joined the Marine Corps. In 1969, I was draft exempt because my draft classification was 'non-defense vital industry.' In other words: oil. I was a third mate on oil tankers, working for Standard Oil of California. My route covered California, Hawaii, Tahiti, and Alaska. It was a very high-paying job, with five months of vacation each year.

Maybe my need to serve and fight was grounded in my samurai heritage. Pictured on the following page is my great-great-great-grandfather, one of the Samurai who greeted Admiral Matthew Perry when Perry opened the doors of trade to Japan. As the first son, of first sons, I am now in possession of the sword in the photo.

My path may also have followed that of five of my uncles who fought in Europe during World War II with the 442 Infantry Japanese-American Battalion, the most highly decorated American battalion in the war. All five came home alive. Or it may have been shaped by another uncle was one of two Japanese-Americans captured by the Japanese and forced to march in the infamous Bataan Death March. Or maybe it was because my younger brother had just volunteered to serve in Vietnam.

When I sat alone on board the oil tanker—a draft-exempt, 21-year-old man earning a lot of money in 1969—my conscience bothered me and spirit took over.

A few months later, I resigned from Standard Oil and reported for the U.S. Navy flight school at Pensacola, Florida. My pay had gone from $4,000 a month to approximately $400 a month. Yet, even then I knew it was one of the best decisions of my life.

Little did I know that my military training was preparing me to become an entrepreneur, a rich and free human being. Today I work hard, not because I need the money, but because I am on a mission, just like I was on a mission in Vietnam. Different missions… but the same spirit.

Can your mission be your freedom? I believe it can.

As an entrepreneur, your first job is to choose your mission. Mission is spiritual, it comes from your heart. Mission is more important than money. Money is important, because money is the fuel of business, but it is your mission that should drive you and sustain you as an entrepreneur. The path can be lonely, frustrating, long, and tough. It can also be challenging, exhilarating and very fulfilling.

Being an entrepreneur is much more difficult than being an employee. The failure rate among entrepreneurs is staggering. I tend to believe that part of the reason for that is that most entrepreneurs did not serve in the military. Your training in the military gives you an incredible head start, an edge. And while it doesn't guarantee success it certainly gives you a strong foundation on which to build.

I don't know of any entrepreneur who has said that the path to success was easy. Most failed many times along the way. I did. Yet it is what I learned at the Academy, in the Marine Corps, in flight school, and in combat—that spiritual toughness—that kept me going… especially when the money was gone and the walls of the business were caving in.

Freedom vs. Security

So the choice is yours, freedom or security? You may find that you need to choose between being an employee or an entrepreneur.

I encourage you to choose for the challenge. Which choice excites your spirit more? Job security or possibility of financial freedom? Neither choice is an easy one today.

Look at what is happening to the middle class… those who are choosing job security:

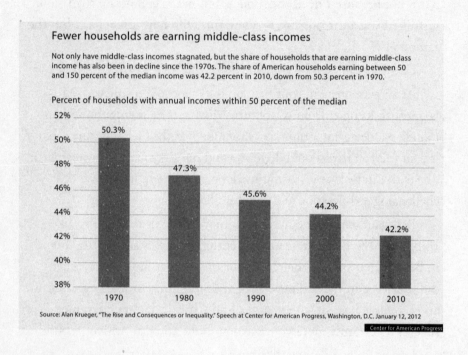

Fewer households are earning middle-class incomes

Not only have middle-class incomes stagnated, but the share of households that are earning middle-class income has also been in decline since the 1970s. The share of American households earning between 50 and 150 percent of the median income was 42.2 percent in 2010, down from 50.3 percent in 1970.

Percent of households with annual incomes within 50 percent of the median

Source: Alan Krueger, "The Rise and Consequences or Inequality." Speech at Center for American Progress, Washington, D.C. January 12, 2012

Center for American Progress

This next chart was used in my book *Second Chance*. You may want to read that book, if you haven't already. It goes into more detail on what entrepreneurs and investors need to learn to become successful.

This chart shows that the middle class are not becoming rich. As the following chart illustrates, they're becoming the working poor sliding into poverty.

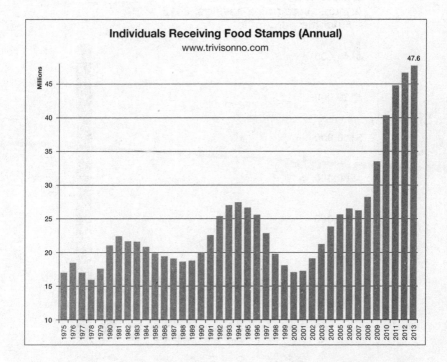

Our politicians claim that poverty is going down in America. What they fail to say is that Food Stamp use is going up among the working poor. As you know, many of our fellow service men and women are on Food Stamps as well as other government programs.

There are several reasons that the gap between the rich and everyone else is getting wider. One of the reasons is that jobs are going over seas. Another is that the rich, those who operate in the B and I quadrants, receive greater tax breaks.

Take a look at the chart below:

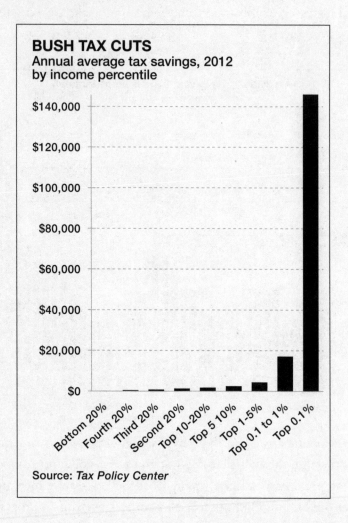

BUSH TAX CUTS
Annual average tax savings, 2012
by income percentile

Source: *Tax Policy Center*

I know what you're thinking. That's not fair.

I never said it was fair. Yet this is what we fight for. You have the same opportunity to be rich—and to enjoy the same tax incentives and tax cuts as the rich.

The hitch? In most cases, you need to be an entrepreneur. Most employees will not qualify for these tax breaks. That is one more reason why the middle class shrinks… and the rich grow richer.

Pictured below is a graph that illustrates who pays the highest percentages in taxes.

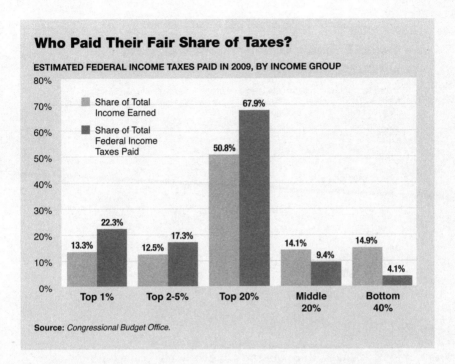

Who Paid Their Fair Share of Taxes?

ESTIMATED FEDERAL INCOME TAXES PAID IN 2009, BY INCOME GROUP

- Share of Total Income Earned
- Share of Total Federal Income Taxes Paid

Top 1%: 13.3%, 22.3%
Top 2-5%: 12.5%, 17.3%
Top 20%: 50.8%, 67.9%
Middle 20%: 14.1%, 9.4%
Bottom 40%: 14.9%, 4.1%

Source: *Congressional Budget Office.*

Among our freedoms is the right to choose our tax rates. We seldom look at it that way, but it's true. These same rights and freedom are available to you and every American. In many countries, these freedoms don't exist.

And remember: these tax incentives are available to anyone, rich or poor, if you qualify. Tax breaks are government tax incentives. For example, the government wants us to own our homes, so we have mortgage tax deduction for homeowners. Entrepreneurs receive more tax breaks than employees, because the government wants entrepreneurs to create jobs.

Ironically, the people who pay the highest taxes are people who have a job, save money, and invest in a 401(k) retirement plan. I know, I know, it's not fair.

Pictured below is what the future seems to holds for Obamacare, the President Barack Obama's Affordable Health Act.

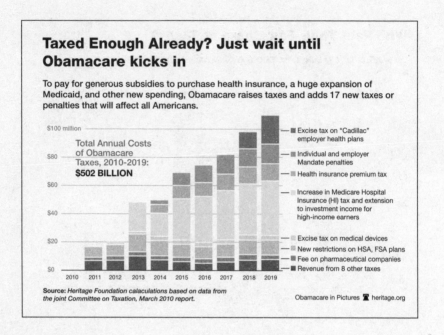

Taxed Enough Already? Just wait until Obamacare kicks in

To pay for generous subsidies to purchase health insurance, a huge expansion of Medicaid, and other new spending, Obamacare raises taxes and adds 17 new taxes or penalties that will affect all Americans.

Total Annual Costs of Obamacare Taxes, 2010-2019: **$502 BILLION**

- Excise tax on "Cadillac" employer health plans
- Individual and employer Mandate penalties
- Health insurance premium tax
- Increase in Medicare Hospital Insurance (HI) tax and extension to investment income for high-income earners
- Excise tax on medical devices
- New restrictions on HSA, FSA plans
- Fee on pharmaceutical companies
- Revenue from 8 other taxes

Source: Heritage Foundation calaculations based on data from the joint Committee on Taxation, March 2010 report.

Obamacare in Pictures ☎ heritage.org

I look at charts like this and I hear myself—at age nine—asking my teacher why we aren't taught about this in school. Money is a part of our everyday lives. And like it or not, our wealth or lack of wealth will have an impact on our future.

I ask the same question today—Why aren't we taught about money in school?—and have become an outspoken advocate for financial education.

It is why Kim and I started The Rich Dad Company. It's why we are committed to bringing financial education—via books and mobile games and board games and apps and new learning platforms—to individuals and families around the world.

Because it's those entrepreneurs who grow businesses in the B quadrant and invest professionally in the I quadrant who make the most money and pay the lower percentages in taxes? The chart below Illustrates that.

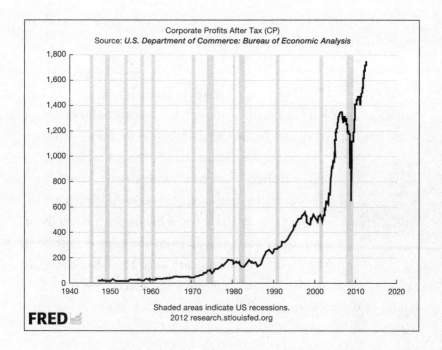

Corporate Profits After Tax (CP)
Source: *U.S. Department of Commerce: Bureau of Economic Analysis*

Shaded areas indicate US recessions.
2012 research.stlouisfed.org

This FRED chart (FRED stands for Federal Reserve Economic Data) shows why the rich are getting richer... very, very rich from profitable businesses Unfortunately, the same can't be said for the poor and middle class.

And this is why I recommend that you consider becoming an entrepreneur.

You joined the military to protect and defend the rights we hold dear, and the right to be rich, poor, or middle class—to be a capitalist, socialist, or communist—is among them.

When I left the Marine Corps in 1974, I chose to be a capitalist. I'm not saying it's been easy, but this is the freedom we fight for and a freedom we defend. We fight for the freedom to be rich—maybe financially free—even if many fellow Americans fight to take those freedoms away.

Since I, and many of you, have fought for the right to be rich or poor, why not be rich? In 1974, when I left the Marine Corps, I decided to become an entrepreneur. I wanted to make a difference in the world. I wanted to challenge myself to see if I could become rich.

We all fight for the freedom to choose the lives we want and the freedom to live our life on our terms.

If you would like to learn more about taxes, I hope you'll tune into the **Rich Dad Radio Show**. I do a weekly radio show, a free hour-long program on financial education for those who want to be rich. We discuss many different topics and many different experts are interviewed. Tom Wheelwright, CPA and Rich Dad Advisor is a frequent guest and if you'd like to learn more about taxes, and how you can enjoy the same tax breaks as the rich, go to ***http://www.richdad.com/radio*** You'll find all of our radio segments archived there. Tom is my tax advisor and the author of the book *Tax-Free Wealth*.

Part Two

★ ★ ★ ★ ★

8 LESSONS IN LEADERSHIP

Chapter Three

LEADERSHIP LESSON #1:
LEADERS ARE ROLE MODELS

War and business are very similar. They are both tough, often dangerous, environments. Many people would love to be entrepreneurs, but lack the skills, courage, and discipline to survive in business. Rather than risk starting their own businesses, most people seek safer environments, preferring job security to freedom and a steady paycheck to greater wealth. Many cling to job security because the fear of failing is greater than the joy of freedom.

Traditional schools prepare students to be employees. Military schools prepare students to be leaders.

Leadership is about being a role model. Leadership is about living one's life to higher standards. Leadership was not just a subject at the U.S. Merchant Marine Academy. It was a process. We had to lead by example, not by textbook philosophies. We had to practice what we were being taught. From early morning until late at night, we were either taking orders or giving orders. If we were not striving to live our lives to higher standards, we were severely reprimanded. Mediocrity and complacency were not tolerated. If we could not take feedback we had no hope of graduating. If we were arrogant, we were soon humbled. If we answered back, we were punished.

The pressure and discipline was intense. And as much as I hated the pressure, I have come to appreciate my four years at the academy. For four years, we were trained to be officers with responsible for multi-million dollar ships, filled with millions of dollars of cargo, and in charge of a large crew doing different jobs on board the ship. That training prepared me for leadership in the world of entrepreneurship.

The B-I Triangle: 8 Essential Elements

The B-I of the B-I Triangle stands for Business and Investor, the B and I on the right side of the CASHFLOW Quadrant. The B-I Triangle is made up of the eight components, integrities, of a business. If a business is struggling or fails, it is because one or more of the 8 Integrities is missing or weak.

Traditional schools focus on the professions that make up the internal triangle of the B-I Triangle: *Product, Legal, Systems, Communications,* and *Cash Flow.*

Military academies focus on the context of the B-I Triangle, the three elements—integrities—that frame the triangle and give it shape and structural integrity: *Mission, Leadership,* and *Team.*

The 8 Integrities of a Business

Traditional schools focus on:

1. **Product:** Primarily its design and development. Most people think the product is the most important aspect of a business. Yet, if you look at the entire B-I Triangle, you will see that product is the smallest component of the triangle—because it's the least important. A product without a strong B-I Triangle behind it will probably not be a successful product.

2. **Legal:** Every business needs attorneys. Attorneys and lawyers are important in protecting your product as well as the rest of your B-I Triangle.

3. **Systems:** A business is a system of systems. A car is also a system of systems, as is the human body. For example, a car requires a fuel system, brake system, electrical system, etc. The human body is made up of the skeletal system, circulatory

system, nervous system, etc. If one system in a business, car, or body is missing or not functioning well, all systems struggle and often fail.

Every business needs professionals trained to operate the systems of a business. Engineers, information technology, manufacturing, marketing, product distribution, and internal business systems fall into this category.

4. **Communication:** A business is all about communication from the top down, to investors, customers, and employees. If communications are poor, so is the company. Professionally, a business needs strong sales, public relations, marketing, web, and human resource communications. Information technology is essential to success in business today.

5. **Cash Flow:** It isn't rocket science to understand that a business must have more cash flowing in than flowing out. A business must have accurate and clear accounting. A business with poor accounting systems is a poor company. That is why businesses require bookkeepers, accountants, and chief financial officers.

Military academies focus on:

1. **Mission:** Mission is spiritual. It is the reason for a company or organization's existence. The first day at the academy, we were required to memorize the mission of the academy and repeat it perfectly. The importance of mission was drilled into our heads from day one.

2. **Team:** Teams represent power. The stronger and more united the team, the more powerful the team. From day one, we were taught how to be members of a team. To be a great leader one must know how to be part of a team. The team is more important than the individual.

3. **Leadership:** Leaders are role models. Leadership is earned. It is earned through trust, respect, experience, and competence.

At the academy, we were trained to operate not as individuals, but as leaders of teams. We were constantly reminded that mission, team, and leadership are essential to operating ships or flying planes into combat. It was drummed into our heads that, in combat, individuals have very little power. Life or death depends upon individuals working as well-led teams. The same is true in business.

Robb's Report by Robb LeCount
follows each of Robert's 8 Lessons

Robb LeCount enlisted in the United States Navy at age 18 and trained as an Aviation Machinist Mate. He's completed a myriad of training including, advanced Power Plants training, weapons training, cold weather survival, and leadership training. His deployments have spanned the globe—from Japan, New Zealand, and the Cayman Islands to Antarctica, to name just a few—and he has served on five U.S. Destroyers and Frigates. Today Robb is the Director of Information Technology at The Rich Dad Company as well as an entrepreneur and small business owner.

Robb's Report

When I enlisted in the Navy I was a misguided punk without a father. I didn't realize it but I was hungry for someone to lead me. That, unfortunately, did not mean that I was going to make it easy on the leader I found.

I immediately found myself in trouble and in the path of my Company Commanders. Yes, we had two Company Commanders. During our Company's study time I thought it would be a great idea to challenge my leader the best way I knew how, by being a smartass.

First, a little backstory on my life. My mother and father divorced when I was five years old and my father moved to the other side of the country. This gave me the unique opportunity to grow up as the man of the house. That's right, the man of the house at the ripe old age of five. My mother did as good a job of raising me as she could. Unfortunately for her she had a very stubborn five-year-old with a Type-A personality. This equated to me not understanding the concept of boundaries, weak discipline, and a complete absence of guidance.

So, our Company compartment was about the size of a small cafeteria, a long rectangular room full of bunks with a center board, a long table for studying, and other activities. My fellow recruits and I were forced to sit on the floor to study—even though there was that giant center board in the middle of the room. Our leader informed us that we had not yet earned the right to sit at the table.

There was to be absolutely no talking or sounds of any sort except pages turning in books and notes being scribbled in our notebooks. It was BORING, but not for long. Our Company Commanders had explained the rules to us, and the length of time we would be studying. Then they went to their office to do whatever it is they did, most likely planning sadistic ways to train us. At least it seemed that way to an 18-year-old with a bad attitude.

I thought this would be a great time for a little humor. After about 10 minutes the room was completely quiet. Guys would not even cough without severely muffling themselves. The silence was killing me and I needed a little fun. I put my head down into my book and mimicked the sound of 'passing gas.' Very loudly, I might add. It was a long, slow squeal and the whole room started to snicker. They couldn't help it. The tension release felt so good, but no one laughed out loud. The fear was too great. I decided to try again. I took a big breath, and had just started to let out the exaggerated sound when… the door opened. Everyone's smiles turned to fear and their laughing eyes were suddenly glued to their books.

One of our Company Commanders, we'll call him Chief Burk, walked in with a stern face and asked, "Who made that sound?" A few seconds went by and he said, "If no one confesses, everyone will be cycled." Being cycled means that everyone lines up, 40 recruits on each side of the center board, and we work out intensely until the Company Commanders feel we learned our lesson. I immediately raised my hand and reported to their office for my punishment.

The next day Chief Burk called me into his office. Walking into his office was intimidating, but I was dead set on not showing any emotion. I was determined not to give this stranger any power over me. I knew he would yell at me and berate me. I was fine with that. I grew up with that kind of behavior from my step dads and teachers all my life. I did not really think about it, but I wanted it. I wanted to see how this authoritative figure would respond. How he would belittle me and cut me down. How he would try to hurt me with his words. I would see how he would try to manipulate me through his power position and I would judge the man. Then I would find his weakness.

But it did not go as I had planned. Chief Burk did not yell at me. Instead he spoke to me as a stern but caring man. And he taught me a valuable lesson. He said, "Seaman Recruit LeCount, there are thousands of Navy recruits on this base. Every one of you is trying to get noticed. There are only two ways for that to happen. You can either give 110% every day and stand out, or, you can be a dirtbag and get set back." Being set back meant that you were sent back to the class behind you and, consequently, extended your training by at least a week. It also meant you had to join an entirely different company, forcing you to learn to work with a different team and a new set of Company Commanders. Other than being kicked out of training, it was the worst punishment you could be given.

Giving 110% every day and being a dirtbag both required a toughness of spirit and stubbornness, but always giving 110% requires a strength only a very few have. It requires the strength of a leader. "Do you know why it is tougher to lead?" he asked me. I wanted to respond with a smart-ass comment. Something like, "'Cause everyone can smell your ass and know you're full of shit," but I refrained. This man had surprised me and I wanted to figure him out before I pushed him further.

Chief Burk continued, "Leaders are praised, but also held to a higher standard, as everyone is watching you and secretly wanting you to fail."

He asked: "Do you know why people want leaders to fail? It's so they have permission to just get by, permission to do what is easy."

He said, "A leader leads by example. A leader dictates the effort and drive of those who follow them."

"You haven't seen the leaders I've had then," I shot off, out of my mouth, before thinking.

"No I haven't," Chief Burk said. "But I think you are confusing being placed in a position of leadership with actually being a leader. Leaders, lead by example. Not through fear and not through the volume of their voice. A leader's power comes from being an example. He earns his leadership. It can never truly be given."

He wasn't done with me yet. "So, Seaman Recruit LeCount, you've got my attention right now, but you did not get it as a leader. I see that you can lead, I see the strength in you. Because of this, I'm going to do two things. I'm going to give you a punishment of running 10 miles before chow. And the second thing I'm going to do is run them with you. When we're done you will tell me if you're going to lead sailors to greatness or give them permission for mediocrity…"

There is more to this story that I will share with you in future the chapters.

So how does this apply outside the military? As an entrepreneur? First off, I am new to this entrepreneur thing. I'm in the process of starting my second business. Let me tell you how leading by example set me up in the work place. After the Navy, I landed a job as a web developer. I was new at the firm and did not know anybody. It didn't matter. I had learned what I needed to do. I needed to set an example. I need to state what I stood for: my ethics, my morals, my beliefs, and my need to be better. From day one I was at work early, and I stayed late. I did not do so to earn points with the boss. I did it because I was being paid a salary and until I was up to speed and producing as much as my coworkers I would not waver.

– Robb LeCount

Chapter Four

LEADERSHIP LESSON #2:
ARE YOU A LONER
OR A LEADER?

The world is filled with people who have good intentions and great ideas. Many have a strong desire to change the world, to make the world a better place to live. They may have great ideas, but in many cases no one listens to them. No one follows. They may be smart, but they have no power. No power to lead or inspire.

Traditional schools train students to be loners, successful on their own. Military schools train student to be leaders, successful only if their team is successful.

One of the toughest jobs at the Merchant Marine Academy was to be the section leader. As section leader, I was in charge of my classmates, my peers—boys about my age. As section leader, it was my job to make sure all my classmates were present and accounted for before we marched to class. Once everyone was assembled, the section leader would say, "Section, attention. Right face. Forward march." As section leader, it was my job to make sure the group marched in step and that no one was goofing around. It was my job to make sure the section arrived to class on time and stayed in class. When the instructor entered the room, the section leader barked, "Section, atten—hut." If any of my section mates broke any of the rules, I was accountable. If a classmate cut class or was late to class, the section leader was punished. (And that was me.) In other words, the section leader got punished *along with* the person who broke the rules. Thank god I was section leader only about once every three months. Keeping 18-year-old boys in line was a very tough job.

In many ways, being section leader helped prepare me for business. Today one of my roles is to keep a group of (so-called) adults—adults who span the age spectrum—in line, accountable, working… and not goofing off.

Rich dad often said, "Business would be easy if it were not for people." I agree. One of the reasons so many people who become entrepreneurs remain small, preferring to be a lone wolf rather than a leader, is because dealing with people, young or old, is never easy. For a business to grow, an entrepreneur must be a better leader, able to deal with more and more people. That takes leadership.

The CASHFLOW® Quadrant

Pictured below is the CASHFLOW Quadrant. *Rich Dad's CASHFLOW Quadrant* is also the title of the second book in the Rich Dad series. Many people report that understanding the CASHFLOW Quadrant dramatically changed their lives.

E Stands for Employee

Employees, whether they are a janitor or the president of a business, often say the same words, "I am looking for a safe, secure, job with a steady paycheck and good benefits."

Most people in the world of business are in the E quadrant. That is because parents often say to their children, "Go to school to get a job." Very few parents recommend, "Become an entrepreneur and start your own business." For most people, job security and a steady paycheck are more important than wealth and financial independence.

In the world of employees, success often means competing against other employees for promotions and pay increases. In many ways, being an employee is living in a dog-eat-dog world, a world where everyone is looking out for themselves. Helping someone get ahead might mean you get left behind, replaced—or fired.

To make matters worse, people in the E quadrant pay the highest percentage in taxes, as compared to those in other quadrants.

S Stands for Small Business, Self-Employed, Specialist… Star, Smart Person, or Solo Act

Many small business owners are loners. Most small business owners have fewer than five employees, if any.

Common phrases heard from people in the S quadrant are:

- "If you want it done right, do it yourself."

- "I want to do things my way. I make my own rules."

- "I am the best. No one can do it better than me."

- "I like my independence. More employees mean more problems."

- "Don't tell me anything. I know what I'm doing."

- "I charge by the hour."

- "I can't do it now. I'm too busy. Maybe I'll be free next week."

One problem with businesses in the S quadrant is that if the S stops working his or her income also stops. For example, if a doctor or dentist goes on vacation, so does their income.

People in the S quadrant are often the lone wolves of business. They value independence. They do not have to be leaders. And people in the S quadrant pay the second highest percentage in taxes.

A B-Quadrant Business Depends upon People, Teams, and Leadership

A B-quadrant business is defined as '500 employees or more.' If leadership is weak within a company of that size, the business suffers or goes bankrupt. If leadership is strong, people, teams, and the business flourish, even in bad times. This is why leadership is essential in the B quadrant.

Common phrases heard from B-quadrant people are:

- "I'm looking for people who are smarter and more experienced than I am."

- "Do they work as a team?"

- "Are they trustworthy?"

- "Can he take feedback?"

- "Does she want more responsibility?"

I-Quadrant People Depend on Return on Investment

Leaders in the B quadrant know how to get people to work to produce more money. Leaders in the I quadrant know how to put *money* to work for them—to produce more money.

Common phrases heard from I-quadrant people are:

- "How do we increase our net operating income?"

- "What is the cap rate?"

- "Are the P/Es realistic?"

- "Can we write covered calls on the stock?"

- "How do we hedge our position?"

Individuals vs. Teams

Many sports are individual sports. Sports such as golf or tennis tend to attract strong individuals. Success in the E and S quadrants generally means being able to survive on your own.

Many sports are team sports. Sports such as football, soccer, rugby, or basketball are team sports. Leadership skills and a strong team are essential for success in the B and I quadrants.

Education at Traditional Schools

Most schools train students to be employees or specialists in the E and S quadrants. Education, in traditional arenas, means studying on your own and competing against your classmates for the best grades. In school, someone is always at the top of the class and someone is always at the bottom. Cooperation is considered cheating. Self-preservation is more important than group preservation. Your classmate is your competition. This attitude often carries over into the corporate world.

Education at Military Schools

Military schools focus on leadership. Students are taught to unite individuals and build teams of people. Upon graduation, students are to lead troops, guide ships, or fly planes. Education focuses on working with different people with different skills and different professions, as well as knowing the entire working systems of a ship or an aircraft. We are taught that the mission is more important than life and a leader's success depends on the success of others. Cooperation and coordination are essential skills of a leader. Personal survival at the expense of others is considered treasonous to the group. At academies, students are taught that *the ultimate sacrifice*, giving your life so others may live, is essential to being a leader.

The B-I Triangle

In the previous lesson on the B-I Triangle, we discussed how military school differs from traditional school. Traditional schools focus on the five *internal* sections of the 8 Integrities of a Business and military schools focus on the *external* three of the 8 integrities.

This is why people in the B and I quadrants have to be competent leaders. Leaders must know how to unite people from different specialties and organize them into productive teams. This means leaders must know how to take people from the E and S quadrants—who have been trained to operate as lone wolves—and train them to operate as part of a team.

This leadership skill is essential to wealth. Since there is often a ceiling on what an E or an S can earn, a leader must be able to get to them operate as a team and produce extraordinary wealth. Cooperation is essential to great wealth.

ACTION STEPS

Exercises to Develop Your Leadership Skills

1. With two or three others, discuss the differences between the four quadrants. Why do people in the E quadrant say, "I'm looking for a safe, secure job with benefits?" Why do people in the S quadrant say, "If you want it done right, do it by yourself?" Why do people in the B quadrant say, "I'm looking for the right people?" And why do people in the I quadrant say, "What is the return on my money and when will it be returned?"

2. Which quadrant are you presently in? What quadrant do you want to be in, in the future?"

3. Discuss loners, people who have great ideas but no one following them. What causes them to be loners?

4. Discuss leaders, those people who others naturally listen to, look up to, and follow. What causes them to be leaders?

5. Discuss times when you are a loner… and when you are a leader.

6. Discuss what you can do to be a better leader. Note: You *can* be a leader in the E and S quadrants.

7. What commitments are you willing to make to improve your skills? Who will hold you accountable? Who will give you feedback?

A Final Word

I was very shy when I first arrived at the Academy. Being in a military school of all men, I found myself being pushed around by men who were smarter, stronger, and more macho than me. It was a tough environment in which to be a leader. Looking back, it was the perfect environment for me… *if* I wanted to develop and become a leader in life.

If I had stayed with my classmates from high school, I would not have been challenged as much as I was challenged at the Academy. If I had stayed with my high school friends, I would probably still be the clown I was in high school. Being forced into positions of leadership every day at the academy taught me to deal with the smart, strong, macho people I would meet in the world of business.

Robb's Report

As you may remember, I had just gotten in trouble for imitating bodily functions with my mouth. Chief Burk had issued his punishment, but also chose to endure my punishment with me. I was to run 10 miles. As we marched to the beginning of the track, I stopped. Chief Burk stopped, too. No one moved. He looked at me, smiled, and began to run. I followed.

We did not talk for the first mile. Chief Burk ran and I followed. Keeping up was difficult. This man was in great shape, especially for someone so much older than me. As we ran I saw the rest of my Company. The other Company Commander had brought them onto the field for their break from school.

Chief Burk slowed down, so I slowed down. The last thing I wanted was to run side-by-side with him and have to engage him in conversation. He slowed down some more. So I did the same. He smirked at me and called to me to catch up and run next to him. I put my head down, cursed at the earth, and did as I was told.

It was obvious that Chief Burk had some things to say to me. "So we know how good you are at anal interpretation. Now let's see how good of a leader you are. I'll make a deal with you. At the end of this lap you can return to the Company. Every member of your company who agrees to run a lap with you is one less lap you have to run."

I was surprised. This sounded like a great deal. But I didn't want to appear grateful.

"You must be getting tired," I said. Again, my smart-ass side speaking before I thought. He smiled at me.

"Do you know how many times I've run these laps?" he asked. "Did you think you were the first to run laps with this old man? I can run laps all day, but what I would like to do is find a leader. THAT would be special. What do you say? Can you lead your squad to giving up their break to run a few laps?"

"You bet," I said. "I'll be right back with just one more lap to run." One thing I wasn't lacking in was confidence.

Chief Burk followed me. I did not expect that, but it didn't matter. He did not place any rules around this and I knew how to get these guys to help me out. We walked up to the nearest recruit...

"Hey, Brackston, let's make a deal." Brackston did not look at me. His eyes were fixed on Chief Burk, looking for some type a signal as to what he should do. Chief gave no such clue. He just impassively stared at me. I spoke again.

"I'll polish your boondockers for you if you'll run one lap with me."

Again. Brackston looked at Chief Burk for some clue as to what he should say. No clue was given.

"Um, no thanks," Brackston said. "I'm just going to hang out and relax."

My shoulders dropped. I needed to sweeten the deal.

"What if I helped you learn the chain of command?" I did my homework before I departed for boot camp and had memorized everything my recruiter had suggested. Needless to say the majority of my company hadn't prepared like I had. This included Brackston, and I knew it.

"No, thanks," Brackston replied, and walked away.

I tried this same routine with three more members of my Company with the same results.

Chief Burk instructed me to start running. I was so confused. How come no one would help me? I was well liked… I thought. We started running again. Now every step was heavy. My spirit was crushed. Just a couple of minutes ago I had been given a way out of this punishment. My spirit was soaring and I thought I was going to get away with my practical joke without receiving any real punishment. Just time with this odd Company Commander.

"Maybe I was wrong about you," he said as he ran in front of me. "Looks like I'm the only leader here. I am the only one with any one following me."

I groaned. This run was now painful. My breathing was heavy, I was hot, and we had just started.

About halfway through the lap Chief spoke again.

"Do you know why you failed?" he asked. I did not reply. I really did not know. I thought I had given each guy a really good offer.

"You did not lead. You did not set an example," he said.

"You merely tried to barter. You did not approach your fellow recruits as a leader, but merely as a salesman. Anyone can say no to a salesman. Who says no to a leader?"

He continued: "A good idea does not make you a leader. A fair trade does not make you a leader. Let try this again, but this time you go back as a leader and speak to them as a leader."

I was silent. I had no idea what that meant. Finally I said, "I am not their leader, we are all equal. This week Harris is section leader."

"I am not talking about section leader. Again you are confusing being placed in a position of leadership with actually being a leader.

Leaders lead by example. Ask yourself what example you can set. What example do they want you to set? What example are you setting right now?" Burk was full of questions.

I was starting to feel an idea coming on. A feeling of warmth entered my brain. I wasn't sure what it was yet, but I was focusing on the words my CC just said, "What example do they want you to set?"

What if these recruits were like me? What would I want? I would want someone just like this strange CC running and enduring my punishment with me. I want to know I always have someone with me when it gets tough. I'd never had that my entire life. What if… what if I gave to these recruits the very thing I'd always wanted? What if by giving it, I could get it back?

This was the weirdest punishment I'd ever received.

"Have you figured it out?" my CC asked. "Are you ready to try again to get your squad to run with you?"

I nodded my head with confidence. This time I went to each recruit and instead of offering bribes, I offered team… and family. I started my conversation with the fact that I messed up. I made a mistake. I followed that with, "If you make a mistake I will be there to help carry the burden. I will help you even if you don't help me. What I want is a team. I want us to be united and look out for each other. I will help you. It's up to you whether or not you want to help me."

Chief Burk was making me a leader. Not a person with passion or courage, but a leader; a man with followers. Do you think it worked? I'll pick this up again in Lesson 6 (Chapter 8)…

– Robb LeCount

Chapter Five

LEADERSHIP LESSON #3: DISCIPLINE DELIVERS A HIGHER QUALITY OF LIFE

How many times have we heard someone say…

- "I need to exercise and lose some weight."

- "I wish I could make more money."

- "How do I get out of debt? These bills are eating me alive."

- "I should start my own business."

- "I need to grow my business."

These are the words of people who know they need to change. They need to improve their lives and move to a higher quality of life. Moving to the next level of life requires more than thoughts, wishes, and hope. It requires discipline. Discipline delivers a higher quality of life.

Many times we become prisoners of our own lives. We are trapped between our problems and our dreams. We know we need to change, but change is not always easy.

Many people do not move to a better life simply because they have become comfortable with their problems. Their problems become their life. For example:

1. A person can be comfortable being overweight because diet and exercise would make them uncomfortable.

2. A person can be comfortable in a job that does not pay enough simply because starting a business would make them very uncomfortable.

3. A person can be comfortable in a relationship that is dead simply because a boring marriage is more comfortable than being alone.

Improving one's life requires discipline. Change often requires that a person be uncomfortable, learn new things, meet new people, and become a better person... *before* the quality of their lives improves. Life does not improve until the *person* improves.

This is why learning discipline—the discipline of discipline—is an extremely important subject taught at military academies.

Traditional schools focus on the discipline of academics; Military schools focus on the discipline of leadership.

I chose a military academy because I knew I lacked discipline. I knew that without discipline I would never graduate and receive a college degree. And although I knew I lacked discipline, I did not learn what discipline really was until I got to the Academy.

At first, I thought *discipline* was what someone did to me. For example: An upperclassman chewing me out—in my face, in front of the world—when I did not follow orders, clean my room, or study at night. After a while, I came to realize that discipline is what I did or did not do *to myself.* It slowly dawned on me that I would never become a leader if I could not discipline myself. I knew people would keep yelling at me until I became more self-disciplined.

The first month at the Academy, many freshmen (aka plebes) could not take the discipline. Many were very smart academically, but could not take the discipline of a military academy. Many could not do even the simplest of things, like getting out of bed when the bugle blew at 0600 or standing for inspection before marching to class. Some did not like being told what uniform to wear or that they needed a haircut. Many could not stand being yelled at when they broke the rules... simple rules such as 'Be early, not late.' Many were spoiled brats at home and were trying to be spoiled brats at the Academy. Spoiled brats did not last through plebe summer, even if they were very smart spoiled brats.

I, too, almost quit the first week. The pressure was so intense I came close to breaking many times. Slowly I adapted and came to understand what discipline really is. Discipline was not about being yelled at. It was not about being scolded, then begrudgingly doing what I was told to do. It was more than that. I learned there are two types of discipline: external and internal. As the days and months passed, I began to realize that external discipline was harshest when I lacked internal discipline. The more I tried to beat the system—cheat, cut corners, lie, disobey orders—the more severe the external discipline.

In other words, I realized that the world is always disciplining us, regardless of whether we want discipline or not. For example, if I were undisciplined with my eating and exercise habits, the world would discipline me. If I were foolish and uneducated with my money, the world would discipline me by taking my money. And If I were a cheat, a crook, and a liar, the honest people of the world would discipline me by avoiding me.

My entire plebe year was hell. I was always assigned to extra-duty. Extra duty was punishment for not following orders. If I was late returning to the Academy, I was given 10 demerits plus an extra demerit for every two minutes I was late. For example, if I were 30 minutes late, I received 25 demerits, 10 just for being late, and 15 extra demerits, one for every two minutes of the 30 minutes I was late. Twenty-five demerits meant 25 hours extra duty. In other words, for every two minutes I was late, I had to work an extra hour at extra-duty. Extra duty could be cleaning toilets, mopping floors, or chipping and painting old pipes. More extra duty for disciplinary problems meant less time at academics.

I was nearly thrown out of school for bad grades and bad conduct. The maximum number of demerits a plebe could receive in a year was 300. If the plebe had over 300 demerits, they were dismissed from the Academy, even if their grades were great. I finished the plebe year with 286 demerits and a 2.01 grade point average.

Slowly, it dawned on me that bad grades and bad conduct were simply the result of a lack of self-discipline on my part.

By the start of my third year at the academy the external discipline began to let up, but only after I became more self-disciplined. It was finally sinking in that if I were to be a leader, I needed a higher standard of discipline, both internally and externally.

Today, older and wiser, I know that when I feel the need to improve the quality of my life—relative to health, wealth, friends, business, and happiness—I know I need more discipline, not less.

Power and the KRC Triangle

The motto of the Marine Corps is *Semper Fidelis*. The verbal version is often abbreviated to *Semper Fi* and translated from Latin, it means: "always faithful" and conveys loyalty and commitment to their fellow Marines.

Semper Fi signified the dedication that individual Marines have to "Corps and country"—and to their fellow Marines. It is a way of life.

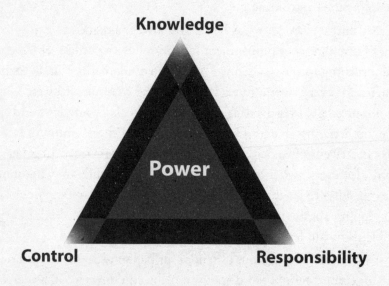

In the Armed Forces there is an interdependent relationship among increasing levels of knowledge, control, and responsibility that coincide with increasing levels of power. A good example of this relationship is the nuclear power Navy or the elite force of Navy Submarines. It is the only place in the United States where a propulsion plant is driven by nuclear power for a vehicle whose sole purpose is to deliver a nuclear warhead when ordered by the nation's Commander-in-Chief. These ballistic missile submarines, or "boomers," serve the function of completing the nuclear triad of air, land, and sea nuclear-strike capability.

The movie *Crimson Tide*, starring Denzel Washington and Gene Hackman, dramatized this responsibility. Without question, the qualification requirements of the officers who command these ships are the most difficult and most respected in the U.S. Navy. Prospective candidates, while still midshipmen, were required to make the drive from Annapolis to Washington D.C. to interview with Admiral Hyman Rickover, the father of the nuclear Navy, to even be considered for the Navy nuclear program. Many never made it through the interview process, let alone the months of schooling that were followed by live-reactor training.

Today Rickover's stringent standards for screening and training remain the most demanding and exacting of any Navy training program. He and the standards he set are credited for the U.S. Navy's record of zero reactor accidents. This record is in stark contrast to the Soviet Union's Navy, which lost several submarines to reactor accidents.

The great responsibility of carrying and potentially launching nuclear bombs carries with it the need for a greater degree of control to ensure compliance with precision standards. With our national security at stake and the unthinkable consequences of making a mistake, any other approach would be reckless. The officers in the U.S. Nuclear Submarine Forces require greater knowledge, more exacting standards, and high levels of control in order to shoulder the awesome responsibility placed upon them by our leaders.

The Four Cornerstones of Discipline: Turning Coal into Diamonds

Pictured below are the four cornerstones of discipline. Each of us has these four components within us.

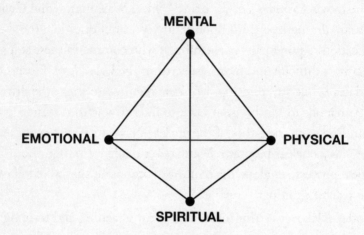

Discipline impacts all four of the cornerstones. Turning coal into diamonds requires pressure, compression, and tension on all four corners.

Many people want to be more successful in life. The problem is they are not strong in all four cornerstones of life. For example, a person may say, mentally, "I need to lose weight." So they go on a diet, which is physical. But three days later, they pass a chocolate brownie and their emotions revolt saying, "I want that brownie. I need my chocolate fix." And the diet is over.

To elevate oneself to a higher quality of life requires strength… mentally, emotionally, physically, and spiritually. When a person fails, or is stuck, or is not able to improve his or her life, it means that one or more of the four cornerstones are weak. It takes the power of discipline to turn the four strengths into a diamond. Without discipline, the four strengths are weaknesses.

Relevant Questions:

1. Why do people work at jobs they don't like?

2. Why do people who want to be rich fail to become rich?

3. Why do so many small businesses fail?

4. Why do so many small businesses stay small?

5. Why do most diets fail?

6. Why don't people exercise?

7. Why do smokers keep smoking?

8. Why do losers keep losing?

9. Why do people cheat and steal?

10. What causes people to be lonely and unhappy?

A Relevant Answer:

A lack of discipline.

Explanation:

Going to the next level of life requires changing mentally, emotionally, physically, and spiritually. This requires discipline. That is why the leadership training at the Academy was life changing for me. The Academy was not just about educating us mentally. Through intense pressure, the Academy transformed us mentally, emotionally, physically, and spiritually.

Returning from Vietnam in 1973 and reentering the real world after nearly 10 years in the world of the military was a cultural shock. I could not believe how undisciplined so many people in business were. I could not believe that people would call in sick when they were not sick, or come to work late, or go home early without telling anyone. I could not believe how excuses, lies, or insubordination was tolerated. If I had done that in the Marine Corps, I would have been shot at dawn—or, at the very least, strongly reprimanded. What disturbed me most was the number of people who were only out for themselves, not caring about their fellow workers or the business. If I had done that as a helicopter pilot in combat, I would have been shot down, propped up, and shot again. Letting a fellow Marine down was not part of the code, the trust, the discipline, the bond among a band of brothers.

Obviously, I had to tone done my Marine-Corps ways and get sloppy with the culture of business. The problem was, I got too sloppy. I relaxed my self-discipline too much. When I found myself failing in business, I knew it was due to a lack of discipline. Through my education at the Academy and in the Marine Corps, I knew there was no one to blame but myself. I knew I had to impose higher standards of discipline on myself before I could improve my life.

Discipline in Business

When a person says, "I can't do it," a leader must quickly assess if the person is lacking mentally, emotionally, physically, or spiritually. A leader needs to know if the person is capable of handling the rigors of what is being asked of them.

Sometimes a person cannot do something because they have not been trained mentally to do it. Or they are physically incapable. Or emotionally deficient and not disciplined enough to handle their fears, anger, or sadness.

In entrepreneurship, all four cornerstones are put under pressure, especially the cornerstone of spirituality. If a person is weak spiritually, all three other cornerstones are weakened. If a person is weak spiritually, it is almost impossible to endure the rigors of entrepreneurship.

Entrepreneurs need all four cornerstones to be successful. An entrepreneur must be able to endure the emotional fears: not having a steady paycheck, continuing to operate when the money is gone, the mental ability to learn quickly especially after making mistakes, the physical strength to work for years without a break, and the maturity to take responsibly for everything associated with the business. And, most importantly, the spiritual strength to be tough in the face of weaknesses in legal, ethical, and moral character and to keep going when all hope is gone. Simply put, character is a function of discipline.

There is no sense asking me to be a computer programmer or web designer. Mentally, I am not trained; emotionally I do not want to learn; physically I could force myself to learn, but I would rather hire a person who is better trained; and spiritually, I am a wimp when it comes to technology.

When I hear a person saying, "How can I invest, I don't have any money?" I need to immediately assess if the person is weak mentally, emotionally, physically, or spiritually. In most cases, the person is weak spiritually. If a person is weak spiritually, then the three other cornerstones are weak as well.

Most of us have heard the saying, "If there is a will… there is a way." When we speak of a person's will, we are speaking of their spirit. In combat, when fear was at its emotional peak, we physically dealt with bullets flying, invisibly, by us. And our minds were desperately flying as well… watching, thinking, shooting, and following orders. If our spirit was weak, we died. If our spiritual strength left us, the four corners came unglued—and people died.

This is what happens to many people who enter the hostile world of entrepreneurship: if they lose their spirit, they lose control mentally, emotionally, and physically. And the business fails. This is why discipline, both internal and external, is essential for facing the hostile environments of war and business. It is both internal and external discipline that keeps a person moving through the tough times and on to the next level of life.

When I say to people that my wife Kim and I were homeless and out of money for over a year, people ask how we survived. Our answer: "It took mental, emotional, physical, and especially spiritual discipline. It was a year that tested our souls, our faith, and our determination to succeed."

Both Kim and I believe that god was testing our spirits. Once god, our maker, or whatever higher power you may (or may not) believe in, knew we would never go back, knew that we would not quit, then "providence moved."

The year 1985 was one of our more memorable years-from-hell. We slept in cars and in friends' basements. We had no money, no work, no car, and often no food. Yet we kept going. Slowly but surely we continued to turn bad luck into good luck. The more often we did that, the more luck—the more magical opportunities and great people—came our way. By 1994, Kim and I were financially free.

Today, we still have our occasional years from hell. We have learned that it is the knowledge that we need to increase the discipline of our four cornerstones that keeps us moving through and beyond our tough times. We know that we need to change before our lives can change.

We continue to work… not for the money, but for the mission. Money is how we keep score. In our line of work, especially, money lets us know if we are practicing what we preach. Our financial statement tells us how good or how poorly we're doing, just as a golfer's score reflects how well he or she is doing. We continue to work at what we think is our best gift. Our mission is to continue to give our gift, to those that want to learn. Even though we have attained wealth beyond our wildest dreams, we continue to test ourselves mentally, emotionally, physically, and spiritually because without daily challenges, we would grow weaker.

Every Day Is Judgment Day

In business, judgment day is not the day you die and meet your maker. Judgment day is everyday, when you meet the real world. For example, if you look at your financial statement and the statement says you are broke, that is judgment day in action. If your wife leaves you for another man, that is judgment day. If more money is flowing out of your hands than is flowing in, that is judgment day. And if money is pouring in, that, too, is judgment day.

What you do with the feedback you get on judgment day is up to you. If you do not like your judgment day report and want to change, that may require mental, emotional, physical, and spiritual discipline.

ACTION STEPS
Exercises to Develop Your Leadership Skills

1. Read this lesson on discipline and leadership and discuss what you've learned.

2. More specifically, what do you know about the four cornerstones and how does discipline affect people mentally, emotionally, physically and spiritually?

3. Have you ever been afraid to say something or do something you knew was important to your life? Which of the four cornerstones were weak?

4. In what areas of your life are you very disciplined and in what areas do you need more discipline?

    Different people have different strengths and weaknesses when it comes to discipline. For example, a person may love to study, so they are disciplined at study. And yet, the same person could be afraid of making mistakes and fail to put into action what they learned from their studies.

5. External discipline is someone with the authority to impose pressure and restrictions on your life. For example, if you want to become healthier, you may hire a fitness coach. Or if you want to become wealthier, you may hire a wealth coach.

    Self-discipline is when you are achieving the success you want on your own. If you find that you want move to a higher level, you may need to hire a tougher coach. This is why most professional athletes have coaches. Pro athletes need to hold themselves to higher standards of performance and achievement. The same is true in business and investing. In other words, amateurs do not use coaches—professionals do.

6. Discuss areas in your life in which you could use more external discipline.

7. What improved levels of life do you want to reach? More specifically, what higher levels of life in the areas of health,

wealth, and happiness? For example, what would you have to do to have more money pouring in and less money going out?

8. How can more discipline assist you in achieving the higher levels of your life?

9. Discuss leaders who have tremendous discipline and leaders who do not. What are the results in each case? For example, President Bill Clinton would have been a greater leader if not for his sexual affairs outside of marriage. Name other leaders who have fallen from power due to moral, ethical, or legal issues.

10. What are the differences between moral, ethical, and legal issues? You may want to use a dictionary to learn the precise definitions of these words before discussing them.

A Final Word

In 1971, I received my wings in Pensacola, Florida. I was officially a professional military pilot. Next stop: Camp Pendleton, California—for guns and rockets—and then on to Vietnam.

The day rockets and machine guns were placed on my aircraft, my life changed again. Sitting on an airstrip at Camp Pendleton, knowing somewhere in Vietnam other young men and women were also preparing for war, put a new perspective on the importance of discipline.

For nine months, the training in California was more intense than flight school in Florida. I had never experienced such pressure, intense pressure to be the best I could be. I needed more discipline because I was preparing for an environment where there is no second best, no second chance. War is not the same environment as in sports contests, where the losers simply pack up their gear and head home. In war, it is kill or be killed. Losers do not go home.

Once again, it was an increase in discipline that took new pilots to new levels of skill, skills essential for survival in the most hostile environment known to man. Today, I use the power of discipline in the world of entrepreneurship, the second most hostile environment known to man—or woman.

I believe all human beings have tremendous untapped power. One of the keys to accessing that power is through discipline. By focusing our mental, physical, emotional, and spiritual powers we can bring out the magical person that lives in each of us.

In closing, discipline is doing what must be done… when it must be done, even when you may not want to do it.

Robb's Report

Robert often talks about military schools teaching the discipline of discipline. I'm sure that's true, but I've found the military mindset as a whole to be my teacher. The military demands discipline. You have no choice. Without discipline in the military, you will suffer and your shipmates will suffer.

It's not just about suffering though. The military forces discipline on you, but it was one of my CCs who made me realize that I was experiencing benefits from my 'buy-in' to the discipline mindset.

My CCs came into our barracks every morning. We would all be terrified and stand at attention, afraid to make eye contact and fearful that a weakness might be exposed. He would walk through our barracks and stop. He would turn and face a random recruit.

"Why did you polish your boondockers that way?" our CC asked the poor recruit.

"To achieve the most optimal shine," came the reply.

"Why do you want your boondockers to shine?"

"Um… to represent the United States Navy the best way possible," the recruit responded with a slight rise in his voice at the end of his statement. He was replying, but almost asking, at the same time, if his response was correct.

Our CC did not break a smile.

"Why?" he continued to ask. And the recruit would answer with the best sounding reply he could think of. The CC would ask the same question again and again and again.

Finally, with the poor recruit's knees about to buckle, he said, "Because if I don't I'll have to run laps around the grinder, sir."

With that the CC would put us all at ease, smile, and walk out.

This happened every morning for a few weeks. We now knew what the CC wanted to hear and would answer his questions the same way everyday: "Because if I don't I'll have to run laps around the grinder, sir."

Until one day… Our CC came into the barracks and asked Seaman Recruit Perry to show the squad his locker, packed with all his uniforms, toiletries, and letters from home. Perry did as he was asked.

"Why is your locker so perfectly organized?" the CC asked.

And it was. Everything was squared up against everything else. The shirts were folded perfectly, and even his letters from his girlfriend were tucked back in their envelope and looked so new it made me wonder if he'd ever read them.

The recruit's reply? You guess it: "Because if I don't I'll have to run laps around the grinder, sir.

"That is not true Seaman Recruit Perry. There is no regulation for managing the inside of your locker."

Perry's face went white. He had no idea what to say. He started to perspire.

The CC showed mercy. "Is it possible, Seaman Recruit Perry, that you have realized that discipline and organization are things to appreciate? That discipline does more than make a great sailor; that it makes a better life?"

The CC just stared at Perry. But as we were all waiting for Perry to answer, I began to think about the question. Had I realized that? Do I think that was true? I did. I saw the value in discipline. It was something that I had committed to. I did not realize it, but now it was so clear. I'd already known that I would always have clean quarters; that I would always fold my uniforms as I was trained. Somewhere I had realized my life was better with discipline and that I was disciplined, not because I was forced to be, but because I wanted that discipline.

– Robb LeCount

Chapter Six

LEADERSHIP LESSON #4:
THE POWER OF RESPECT

The lion is known as the King of the Jungle. Lions are known for their strength, and feared and respected for their power. Although solitary lions are ferocious, when they hunt, they hunt as a team, a pack, also know as a pride of lions.

Leopards are also feared and respected. The reason they may not be known as the 'kings of the jungle' is because they generally hunt with stealth, cunning, and silence, and generally as solitary predators.

Traditional schools focus on the student becoming strong as an individual. Students take tests on their own and cooperation is considered cheating. Schools reinforce the idea that life is about the survival of the fittest... the fittest *individual*. Weaker students are to be eliminated, treated as a sub-species, not fit to climb the ladders of power. Getting the highest grades is preparation for the dog-eat-dog world of climbing your way to the top, alone.

Traditional schools focus on training students to be leopards. The kings of industry and commerce, in most cases, chose an education path that trained them to be lions, generalists who became leaders of teams destined for success.

Military education begins by breaking down an individual and then rebuilding them mentally, emotionally, physically, and spiritually. Then these men and women are trained to operate as a team, to be of service to god and country.

In the military, especially on ships and aircraft, it is tough to isolate oneself from contact with others. In such confined quarters, respect is essential to cooperation. In battle, respect is more important than rank, which is why respect is an important subject at military schools.

Respect is essential to personal and organizational pride. Military academies focus on training students to be lions.

Respect was a very important subject at the Academy and in the Marine Corps. As plebes, we were immediately taught to respect upperclassmen, even if we were all about the same age... between 17 and 21 years old.

Disrespect was a more important subject. Disrespect toward anyone, was not tolerated. Disrespect was more than an infraction... it was almost a sin. Disrespect was severely punished. We were taught to respect those above us, equal to us, and those below us. Although there were no women at the Academy, we took classes on how to be officers and gentlemen, especially when it came to the treatment of women. We even had classes on how to eat with proper etiquette... the proper way to hold a knife and fork, offer a toast, and how to hold a lively, yet respectful, conversation at the dinner table.

Respect and disrespect were very tough subjects, especially for teenage boys. As a young boy, disrespect was cool. Mouthing-off and giving-lip to others was extra cool. Respecting others meant you were a wimp or a butt-kisser. This struggle between respect and disrespect was a very big subject at the Academy and in the Marines.

In combat, the lessons of respect and disrespect paid off. In combat, officers who did not have the respect of their troops often died, some shot from behind. In combat, I learned that a Marine private was just as important as a Marine general.

When I entered the business world in 1974, I was shocked at the amount of disrespect that was tolerated. In business, many times the better managers were perceived to be the managers who were most disrespectful to their workers.

Today I read about managers complaining about the lack of respect from their workers. Well an applicable lesson from military school is this; Respect has to be given before it is received. Giving respect and being sensitive to any aspect of disrespect was an essential part of my military education. Respect builds pride and pride is essential to lions, humans, and organizations.

Respect is essential to leaders and leadership.

ABC: Always Be Caring

In the world of sales, ABC stands for Always Be Closing. In other words: diffuse objections as you 'ask for the order.'

Most people have experienced a salesman's hard sell. Most people find it offensive. Yet hard selling, the ABC formula of 'always be closing,' is what is taught in most sales trainings.

While it is important to be asking for the order, most successful salespeople know that closing is easier if the customer knows you care about them. No one likes a salesperson who thinks more about their commission than the needs of the customer.

In the military world, ABC stands for Always Be Caring. A soldier will respond, even to harsh and tough reprimands, if the soldier knows the reprimand is for their own good and the good of the team and the mission.

In the military the order of caring is:

1. Mission

2. Team

3. Individual

In business the order of caring too often is:

1. WIIFM… What's in it for me.

The Power of Feedback

At the Academy, we were trained to give feedback as well as receive it. Being told what you're doing wrong on a daily basis can break you down, if you let it get to you. Severe criticism is not easy to take, so we were trained to understand its value and to take it.

Learning to take severe and harsh criticism made us stronger, more self-confident, better able to learn quickly and capable of not taking the reprimand personally. We learned to hear the feedback without reacting emotionally. We were trained to not let criticism hurt our feelings, but instead to use it to build a stronger mind, body, and spirit.

Once we learned to take feedback, we were then trained to give feedback. In many ways, I found that giving feedback was tougher. Giving feedback or criticism was not just about yelling at someone. We had to learn to give feedback in many different ways. Regardless of whether we were yelling, mocking, or harassing, we had to let the person know we cared—for the person, team, and mission. Without caring, criticism triggered anger, built resentment, and often backfired on the leader.

One of my instructors once said, "Whether you are praising or reprimanding, never forget to be caring. Before you rip into someone, you must first find compassion in your heart for your fellow human being. Communication is easier with a bridge of caring." This has been a lesson I have used throughout my military career and in business. I believe it was this lesson that brought my crew home from the war. I believe it is this lesson that creates success in business. When I am selling, I do my best to remember to 'always be caring.' Even when I have to fire someone, I do my best to do it in a way that shows compassion.

It is sad that the term "going postal" has become a joke, a punch line. I suspect one reason we have many more incidents of mass murder in business and on school campuses is due to lack of respect, a lack of caring, and poor leadership.

At the academy and in the Marine Corps, it was constantly reinforced that leaders care more about others than they cared about themselves.

Leadership Is a Function of Communication

Pictured below is the B-I Triangle, the 8 Integrities of a Business, with a focus on the areas of communication and leadership.

Simply said, "Leadership is a function of communication And the better the communicator, the better the leader, and the stronger the organization."

In reality, the entire B-I Triangle is about communication. For example, lawyers go to school to learn the language of law. Systems engineers go to school to learn the language of engineering. Accountants go to school to learn the language of finance and cash flow. And marketing people speak the language of sales and marketing. And that is the problem: Each of the five core specialties of the B-I Triangle, from product to cash flow, all speak different languages. Marketing people do not know how to speak to accountants and lawyers do not know how to speak to product design people. For a business to survive and thrive, all five, core specialties of the B-I Triangle must learn to communicate, and this is where the role of leadership is mission critical.

The exterior of the B-I Triangle is made up of three elements, all critical to an organization's ability to hold its shape, its structural integrity. These three important elements are mission, leadership, and team.

When it comes to communications, a leader has two important tasks.

They are:

1. The leader must insist on respect and caring for others in all communications throughout the organization as well as outside the organization. Without respect and caring as the carrier wave of communication there is an extra level of inbred discontent, anger, and infighting within the organization. Without respect and caring, customers find a new company with which to do business. Again, this does not mean the leader needs to be sugary sweet and phony. A leader must be real, sincere, and caring, even if he or she is angry.

2. A leader must know the language of the five core specialties as well as the language of mission, team, and leadership. For example, a leader must understand the marketing function and language, as well as the role of legal and its language… and on and on. In other words, a leader must know a little about a lot and be respectful of what others know and what the leader does not know.

In most business organizations, there is always some disharmony between each professional specialty. For example marketing people often struggle to communicate with legal people, and so on. This is why leaders need to enforce caring and respectful communications throughout the organization, without favoring one specialty over the other. Simply said, a leader does not need to know everything, as long as they are respectful and caring for the entire organization and the people the organization serves.

One problem with promoting the head of accounting, legal, systems, or marketing to leadership over the entire organization is they tend to favor their specialty and minimize the importance of the other professional specialties.

One last point I want to make here is this: leaders do not have to know everything… as long as they remain respectful and caring for the good of all. Leaders and entrepreneurs are generalists who surround themselves which specialists who bring precise, area-specific knowledge and experience to the team.

At the Academy, in preparation for leadership roles, we were required to know everything about a ship. I had to understand the engine room and be able to speak to the engineers. During our year at sea, we were required to spend a number of hours each day actually steering the ship, so we could gain a sense of how a ship rolls and pitches through the ocean. While in port, students studied dockside operations, refueling, replenishing food and water in foreign ports, international law, and loading and unloading cargo.

For four years, it was drummed into our heads that leadership is a function of communications. During our plebe year, we studied Morse Code, so we could communicate to other ships via blinking lights. We also studied semaphore, communication via hand-held flags. We were required to know how to communicate, via ship's flags, our status and position. For example, a red flag on the mast meant we were hazardous, probably taking on fuel.

When I entered flight school, the process was the same. Before we were allowed to fly, we had to know the plane and the organization required to keep the plane in the air. As student pilots we had to learn how to speak to the radio specialists, metal and airframe repair specialists, jet engine mechanics, and guns and rocket specialists. Leadership was about language and communication with caring and respect. Caring and respect were especially important for pilots, if we wanted to have a plane that would keep flying.

Team and Respect

From day one, we are trained to march in formation, in step, following orders as a team. In combat, we hunted as a team. If one of us went down, we stayed with the downed crew member as long as we could. Deserting a teammate in trouble was more than a crime, it was a spiritual sin. It was against our code.

As Marines, we all knew what it was like to be on the ground with a rifle. We understood what the guy on the ground was going through. We knew how they felt and that made us, as pilots, more of a team with the guys on the ground.

One very demoralizing aspect of combat was asking permission to shoot. On a number of occasions, before we as pilots could fire, we had to call a central control center for permission to fire. Nothing was more demoralizing than saying, "Bad guys in sight. Request permission to engage."

And then the voice on the other end, like the voice of god, would say, "Wait one."

"Wait one?" I'd scream back. "The guys are running. They'll be gone in five seconds."

"Cannot grant permission. Wait one," was the reply.

In no time the bad guys were gone, allowed to live and to kill another day… simply because I had to ask permission to fire.

Later I would find out that on some missions, when requesting permission to fire, permission had to come from some civil servant in Washington. Today, I get sick at the thought that our presidents—Bill Clinton, George W. Bush, and Barack Obama—have had no military experience, yet they have the power to send young men and women to war.

In business, I get just as sick when accountants, attorneys, web designers, or engineers, professions without any front-line business experience, make decisions in a vacuum.

Today, too many of our leaders in politics, academics, business, and religion are making decisions from the ivory towers of inexperience. Too many academically smart people have forgotten what it is like to be on the front lines and their decisions reflect this lack of real-world experience.

As a leader of my business today, I never forget the troops on the front line. I never forget that my job is to keep them and our customers alive.

ACTION STEPS

Exercises to Develop Your Leadership Skills

1. Discuss the character trait differences between lions and leopards and why lions are called the Kings of the Jungle.

2. Why is ABC, Always Be Caring, important in communication, even in anger?

3. Why is respect more important for lions than for leopards?

4. Why is leadership a function of communication skills?

5. Why do military schools focus on teaching students to know a little about everything and traditional schools focus on students knowing a lot about a little?

6. How are military school education and an entrepreneur's education similar?

7. What are you best suited to be… a lion or a leopard?

8. How can you improve your communication skills?

9. How can you be a stronger communicator and still be more caring?

10. When angry or when you need to correct someone, how can you be more caring… before communicating?

At military school it was drilled in to us to be respectful.

1. Recall a time when someone was respectful toward you and how it made you feel. Recall a time when someone was disrespectful toward you and how that made you feel.

2. Recall a time when you were respectful toward someone and how it made you feel. Recall a time when you were disrespectful toward someone and how that made you feel.

3. Discuss the power of respect and disrespect.
   (The point is that if you are respectful, the sun and the moon will come to you but if you are not respectful, it can cost you.)

4. What is the price one pays, in business, for being disrespectful? What is the reward for being respectful?

A Final Word

At the Academy and in the Marine Corps, I learned the incredible power of respect and the horrifying consequences of disrespect.

As a pilot on the front line, I gained a deep respect for my men as well as a deep respect for the enemy. I personally did not hate the North Vietnamese or the Viet Cong. I understood why they fought so hard, even though the United States had superior weapons and technology. In my opinion, one of the reasons we lost that war was because our leaders did not respect the enemy. Our leaders were arrogant, removed from the front lines, out of touch with reality, and disrespectful of the spiritual will of the enemy. I see us doing the same thing in the Middle East today.

Robb's Report

Respect is so powerful. In a few chapters we'll discuss unity. I think respect is the foundation for unity, so it may be one of the most important elements of leadership.

Respect is a symbiotic relationship. Do you respect someone and then bond with them? Or do you share a bond that grows into respect? I believe it's both. Respect is fluid.

So far, I've shared some positive stories about some great leadership. The military creates great leaders, but even in the military someone may receive a position of leadership that and had not earned. When that happens do you give them respect? Do you respect the position, even if you can't respect the person?

As a civilian you have the luxury of choice when it comes to respect for people. In the military you have to respect the rank even if you don't respect the individual. That's what provides the fundamental structure in the military, the chain of command. And the chain of command needs to be respected. It's a punishable offense to disrespect a higher-ranking sailor.

I respect people, more than titles. So when I encountered a Maintenance Officer that I could not respect I did not show him respect because of his title. I was in a unit that I respected though. So out of respect for my unit and respect for myself I did not disrespect my Maintenance Officer. I did not show him respect, but I didn't show him disrespect either.

I respected the choice to live a life of discipline. I respected my unit that had made the same choice and commitments that I had. Because of a life full of respect, my actions stayed the same, even with an unrespectable leader. Until… I was on deployment to Antarctica. My squadron was like family. We had a code we lived by in addition to the code of the military. We looked out for one another. We constantly challenged one another, and when one failed we all shared the consequences.

It was three months into our deployment and our Maintenance Officer was re-assigned to a new unit, and a replacement MO was sent in his place. I learned something here. When the military has a bad leader… they ship him far, far away… unfortunately (in this case) to my duty station in Antarctica.

Robert has said, "In the military world, ABC stands for Always Be Caring. A soldier will respond, even to harsh and tough reprimands, if the soldier knows the reprimand is for his or her own good and the good of the team and the mission.

In the military the order of caring is:

1. Mission

2. Team

3. Individual

My new MO did not care about anything but himself. He started barking orders that were very dangerous, changing policies and processes. In Antarctica there is a very specific way to do things. The harsh climate and hazardous situations demanded that we needed to be very careful, very methodical. The new MO never took the time or energy to learn these things and began making very dangerous decisions.

I could not obey. Unfortunately respect has to be earned. It is not a gift. This MO did not earn my respect. Maybe he had earned respect in the past, but if he was relying on past actions to gain current respect, then he was in trouble. I firmly believe that respect is not earned through any single action, but through a lifetime of actions.

This new MO was placing the mission, the team, and me in jeopardy. It was a tough situation. I got together with a couple of guys from other shops and we tried to figure out what to do. We decided as a group that the protecting the Mission, the Team and our Lives was more important than the fear of punishment.

We made the right call. We respected the things that deserved respect. Our new MO quickly, by violating the squadron's rules, got bitten by the cold and sent back to the states for medical care and retraining. No one, ever, wants 'retraining.'

– Robb LeCount

Chapter Seven

LEADERSHIP LESSON #5:
THE NEED FOR SPEED

When you walk into a McDonald's fast food restaurant and say, "I'll have a Big Mac, Chicken McNuggets, two orders of fries, one small and one super-sized, a large diet Coke and a medium regular Coke," how long do you expect to wait? Two minutes? Five minutes? Ten minutes?

If it took 30 minutes, what would you do? Would you wait patiently? Would you complain? Would you go to Burger King?

What if the clerk said, "I'm sorry, we're out of fries. Would you like rice instead?" What would you do? How would you react?

In today's ultra-fast world, a leader must be able to manage and master the controls of organizational speed.

Today, people and organizations that are slow are obsolete—and soon out of business.

During World War II, German submarines torpedoed millions of tons of merchant ships carrying cargo to Europe for the war. This forced the U.S. Merchant Marine Academy to train ships' officers to sail, not as individual ships, but in convoys of merchant ships, protected by U.S. Navy warships. The problem was; A convoy of ships could go only as fast as the slowest ship.

At the Academy, leadership training involved not only leadership of your ship, but the orderly and precise movements of many ships. We had one instructor who set out for Europe in three convoys and never made it. His ship was torpedoed three times in World War II. The convoy went on but he was sent back to the U.S. after being rescued. He said, "There is nothing more frustrating than to be on a fast ship, but be held back because we could only travel as fast as the slowest ship. I hated being a sitting duck. We wanted to use our speed to run, but we had to maintain the same speed as the slowest ships: He went on to say: "I still have nightmares of a torpedo piercing the side of my ship, followed by a deathly silence… then the explosion." He was one of our best and most interesting instructors. Through him, we gained respect for the importance of organizational speeds.

Today, millions of jobs have been lost because many business leaders are too slow. Look at General Motors as an example. For years they were the world's largest auto maker. Where are they today? Corporate and union leaders failed to adjust to a changing world. Bankruptcies… bailouts… a struggle to keep pace, and stay profitable, in a fast-paced, ever-changing world. The costs, measured in human losses as well as financial losses, have been extreme. As the saying goes, "You snooze, you lose."

The Four Organizational Speeds

Military and entrepreneurial leaders need to be in control of four different types of organizational speeds:

1. Angular speed

2. Process speed

3. Pocket speed

4. Gradient speed

The following are simple explanations of each type of speed. Following the explanations are physical exercises you can do to better understand each type of speed.

Angular Speed

The earth orbiting the sun is an example of angular speed. Without angular speed, the earth would stop rotating and fall into the sun.

Exercise: There are five steps to experience angular speed physically.

Step 1. Take a piece of string and tie a weight, such as a washer, to the end of the string, as pictured below.

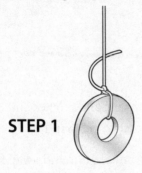

STEP 1

Step 2. Grip the string in the middle and rotate the washer.

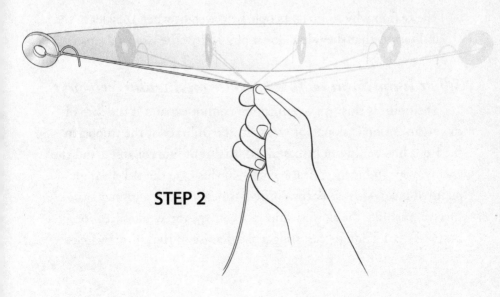

STEP 2

Step 3. Once washer is rotating at maximum distance from your fingers, relax your hand and let the hand rotate.

STEP 3

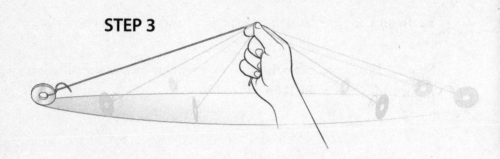

You may notice that when your hand relaxes and begins to rotate, the washer drops and comes closer to the hand.

Step 4. To get the washer to rotate out and away from your hand, your hand must rotate at less of an arc and rotates at a frequency—high speed—of rotation.

Step 5. The arc of the washer can be expanded as long the hand rotates in a smaller arc and at a higher frequency.

The reason why so many people gain weight when they leave the military is that they slow down physically. Their *speed* drops.

What Is the Point to This Exercise on Angular Velocity?

The point is this: An organization cannot expand if the core of the organization is sloppy or weak. In the military, if the troops on the front line could not be sustained, the front line collapsed and the enemy won. In business, if the core—in this case the B-I Triangle pictured below—is weak the entire business is weak and may not survive. Just like the slowest ship in a convoy, the weakest section of a business's B-I Triangle can trigger the demise of the entire business.

If the B-I Triangle of a business is weak, sloppy, or without strong internal controls and communications, the organization cannot expand and grow.

Internal controls and strong internal cooperation is essential among the disciplines within the B-I Triangle—the 8 integrities of a business—before a business can expand. McDonald's is able to expand to a worldwide organization because it has a strong internal business core with excellent leadership.

Most small businesses stay small because the business owner is the one and only core component. To grow, a small business leader must build a team around the B-I Triangle, build in strong internal controls and communication systems, and be a leader who can keep the core of the business strong and working in harmony.

Process Speed

When you order a Big Mac from McDonald's, the length of time you wait for the burger is process speed. The important point to remember related to process speeds is how far back in time does the process go? How much planning did it take for that burger to reach you? That is an example of process speed.

Time is money. In business, many businesses fail because their process speed is too slow. Many people are obsolete because their process speed is too slow. The slower the process the more money it takes to stay in business.

> **Exercise:** Get a watch (or check your cell phone) and note the time. Then drive to your local supermarket, buy some hamburger, a bun, lettuce, and tomatoes. Then drive home, grill the hamburger, and put the burger on the bun with lettuce and sliced tomato. Clean up the mess.
>
> **Questions:**
>
> • How long did the process take?
>
> • How much did the raw ingredients cost?
>
> • If you pay yourself $10 an hour labor, how much did labor cost?
>
> • How much does transportation and clean-up cost for one burger?
>
> • What is the total cost and how long did the process take?

Most people can prepare a better hamburger than McDonald's. But very few people can build a better business process, a process that operates 24/7 around the world, producing and delivering millions of burgers, Cokes, and French fries a day. That is an example of process speed.

For most of us, waiting longer than five minutes for our fast food will be inconsistent with "fast food." We go somewhere else. That is why process speed as individuals and organizations is an essential component of leadership.

Pocket Speed

Pocket speed is the ability to hit a target in time and space.

Exercise: Find a pool table. Place a ball in the middle of the table and take a shot at a corner pocket.

If the ball is hit too far to the left, the ball misses the target. Too far to the right, it misses the target. Hit it too hard, and the ball hits the pocket and jumps out. Hit too soft, the ball may be on target, but comes up short.

In naval operations, officers are trained to operate their ship as well as coordinate their ship with a squadron of ships. The objective of the squadron leaders is to get ships, troops, aircraft, and artillery to a place and time in the future, ready to fight.

In business, leaders focus on coordinating people, time, money, and resources with events in the future. For example, a business is going to put on a seminar for 1,000 people, six months from today. Immediately, the leader must coordinate every component of the B-I Triangle to hit a target six months in the future. If coordination is late, the business misses its target. If the business doesn't spend enough time, money, people, and resources to promote the event, fewer than 1,000 people will show up. If the event planning is poorly executed, those people may show up to a shoddy event. This is an example of pocket speed in business.

Gradient Speed

How fast a person learns is an example of gradient speed. For example, how long does it take for a baby to learn to walk? How long after learning to walk will it take for a baby to run a mile?

Different people learn and adapt at different speeds. Depending upon the subject, different people learn different subjects at different speeds. Controlling these speeds is an essential component of leadership.

Exercise: Learning to brush your teeth. If you are right-handed, start brushing your teeth with your left hand. How long will it take for you to be as good at brushing your teeth with your left hand as you are with your right hand? This exercise will give you an example of gradient speed. Leaders must be vigilant on gradient speeds—of individuals as well as of the entire organization.

Putting the Four Speeds Together

Leaders must be instinctively aware of all four speeds operating simultaneously. Take a moment to think about how incredibly organized McDonald's must be to operate all over the world. That is an example of *angular speed,* speed that requires a strong business core, a strong B-I Triangle.

Then think about how long it takes for McDonald's to deliver you a burger, fries, and soft drink, after you place your order. That is an example of *process speed*.

Imagine how far back, in time and distance, the coordination began so that the burger, fries, and soft drink would be ready for you to order. In other words, how much lead time did it take to get the beef and buns to the store? This is an example of pocket speed.

Now think about how long it takes to train a new franchisee, management team, and workers to run an efficient McDonald's? That is an example of gradient speed. Gradient speed is not only how fast people can learn, but also the effectiveness of the teachers?

Effective leaders are constantly improving their skills in monitoring and controlling these four organizational speeds.

In late 1972, the NVA, the North Vietnamese Army, broke through the DMZ, the demilitarized zone that divided North and South Vietnam. We all knew that, if not stopped, the NVA would roll to Saigon and the war would be over.

The United States organized a combined-forces operation, a last ditch effort to stop the NVA. The operation required the coordination of the Air Force, Navy, Army, and Marines. On the day the offensive started, Air Force B-52 bombers pounded the area with tons of bombs. The Navy ships shelled the area as the bombs were dropping. Once they were through, the Army and Marine helicopters picked up South Vietnamese Army and Marines and began taking them in hot landing zones. The combined operation was a disaster.

First of all, the Air Force, Navy, Army, and Marine leaders could not get their acts together. Angular speed was jeopardized. Secondly, the Air Force and Navy ordnance missed their targets. Process and pocket speed was compromised. When the Army and Marine helicopters were entering the zone, someone misread the maps and landed the troops—not in the designated landing zone, but in the headquarters of the NVA, their most heavily fortified area. Sixteen helicopters were shot down and over 60 South Vietnamese soldiers lost their lives as helicopters crashed and burned. Gradient speed slowed. The NVA had been fighting for years. They had far more experience and were better prepared. For most Americans, we were new to the war and couldn't wait to go home.

Action Steps
Exercises to Develop Your Leadership Skills

1. Discuss each of the four speeds: angular, process, pocket, and gradient.

2. How are they important in business and in life?

3. What happens to people and businesses that cannot control the four speeds?

4. What happens to organizations when some people work slowly and others work faster?

5. How does speed affect profits?

6. When it comes to the four speeds, why is it difficult for a small mom-and-pop hamburger business to compete with McDonald's?

7. Even if a mom-and-pop hamburger operation works very hard, why would McDonald's still beat them financially... even if mom and pop made a better hamburger?

Planning Exercises:

1. Plan an event sometime in the future. If you are a CASHFLOW Club leader, plan a special event.

2. Charge money. This makes the task harder and better.

3. Prepare marketing and promotional plans. This focuses your ability to communicate value.

4. Organize a team to support event.

5. Put on the event.

6. Debrief the event with your team, if you actually put on the event.

7. While debriefing, discuss the four speeds.

   a. **Angular speed:** How well did the team function? How effective was the leadership? How clear were the internal communications? How clear were the tasks?

   b. **Process speed:** How well synchronized were the team, tasks, and process? What could have been improved? How did people respond to the invitation or advertising? Was the communication to potential customers clear? What could have been improved?

c. **Pocket speed:** How well defined was the target? How were the speeds? Was there enough support to make the event happen? Were the efforts too weak or too strong?

d. **Gradient speed:** Was the team experienced enough to make the event successful? What experience was lacking? What was the experience gained? What can be done to make the next event more successful?

Additional exercise: If you do not want to put on an actual event, discuss the reasons why. You might not be ready to be a leader. You may want to reduce the gradient speed and operate as a team member for a few events. Remember, leadership is a learned skill. The military invests years developing its leaders. It is up to you to seek your level of gradient speed.

When discussing your reasons for not wanting to take on a role of leadership, refer back to Leadership Lesson 3, the lesson on discipline. When someone is afraid or hesitant, remember the four cornerstones.

They are:

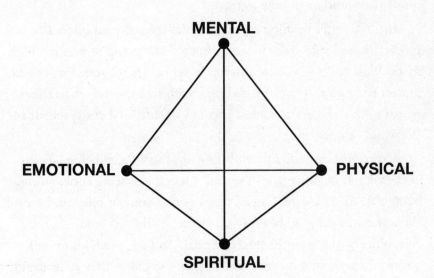

If you are hesitant or simply refuse to do an exercise, a test of your leadership skills, ask yourself where the pressure is. Is it mental (not having the experience), emotional, (not controlling doubt and fear), physical, (not allowing the time), or spiritual, (simply not something you want to do with your life)?

A Final Word

One reason I did not like traditional schools was the practice of punishing students for making mistakes. How can anyone learn anything if they do not make mistakes—*many* mistakes? Each one carries a lesson, an opportunity to learn.

In military school, we had tough academic requirements. We were also required to take what we learned and put our education into action. I would never have learned to lead men, drive a ship, or fly a plane if I was not willing to make mistakes and learn from them. None of us is born walking, talking, or riding a bike. We have to practice and make mistakes if we want to learn. I was not born a leader. I had to practice leading my classmates around the school. I was not born a leader of a ship. I had to spend years practicing to drive ships to far away lands. I was not born a pilot. I had to climb into a plane and learn how to fly.

In 1972, after pushing my boundaries mentally, emotionally, physically, and spiritually in war, I knew I was going to beat my high school classmates who were smarter in school than I was. I was going to beat their good grades by making much more money than they ever would. I was going to beat them as a leader and entrepreneur in the world of business.

I know this sounds silly and childish. But I hated being labeled as stupid and incompetent in school. I hated not being cool and not being able to get a date. Once I flew my first combat mission, I found the way I was going to beat my classmates... the "A" students, the class officers, the 'most likely to succeed,' and the prom kings and queens. I was going to beat them by going to places they were afraid to go and doing things they were afraid to do. To do that, I needed to develop my mental, emotional, physical, and spiritual strengths, the strengths required to do what most people will not do.

So for those of you who do not want to put on a simple event to test your ability to lead people, for whatever reason, you are probably missing an opportunity of a lifetime. Life and personal development is about taking on new challenges for personal growth. Unfortunately, for most people life is about security, safety, and weekends off. That is the difference between those who lead and those who follow. When they play the game of life, they're playing 'not to lose'—versus playing full-out... playing to win.

Robb's Report

This chapter has a lot of meaning for me. The lesson here is that you are only as strong as your weakest link. Robert talks about the effect of a weak link in the military or in business. It's a tough situation. What's a leader to do when he or she identifies the weak link?

I am a leader. This means people follow me. This means I have a team. What do I do if a team member is hurting the team? There is not one right answer to this question. It will always depend on the situation. But there are some things I learned in the military by being a part of a strong, unified team.

Sometimes a unified team doesn't always win. That sounds odd doesn't it? Being unified is a MAJOR piece of winning, but there are other elements too. The element I'm talking about is assigning the right people to the job they are best suited for.

I've written about my team in Antarctica, and it was a true honor to be involved with such great sailors who came together and performed at 110%—all day, every day. We logged insane amounts of operational flight hours, we had an impeccable safety record, and we were always one step ahead of the needs of our command.

I am so proud of that team. We were family. We were united. But... in the beginning we were slow. Our unit was plagued with constant mechanical breakdowns and most of us had just begun working together. Luckily, we had a few things going for us: We all had a great respect for our jobs and we'd all been trained very well to do our jobs. But some of us were fulfilling functions that were not well suited to our natural abilities.

We talked all the time. We were able and allowed to be honest with each other. This freedom to communicate and always tell the truth led to our success. As a leader, I called a team meeting. I asked the team to rate their own performance and their satisfaction. The team validated what the numbers had shown. We had four members out of place.

Two of our senior mechanics were less efficient than the rest of the team. They wanted to be faster and tried everything they could, but that was not their gift. At the same time, two of our quality assurance inspectors were bored. They never would have complained, but we came together as a team to speak honestly. The solution was clear. The mechanics with the most knowledge took on the quality assurance functions and the other 'bored' mechanics began working with their hands.

The uptick in performance was evident almost overnight. When you have team members of great quality, the trick is not eliminating them but finding where they can be most productive. By having respect for the mission first, team second and self third, the conversations that needed to take place were possible and took us to a higher level.

That was not where we stopped though. We wanted to be even better. We began having these honest talks weekly. Every week we'd identify our weakest link—or links. We did not do it to bash guys or make them feel bad, but to teach them. We'd share tricks that other team members had learned. We made each other better.

One week it was my turn. I was always a little slow when it came to safety wiring fasteners. We did those repairs a lot, and they were extremely important because it was what stops bolts that hold vital components in place from coming loose and falling off. Needless to say, with some coaching from a shipmate and a little practice, I was safety wiring with the best of them. I was made better. I had to be open to accepting the feedback and, when I did, I became better for it. Truth is, it's easier to accept feedback, then it is to give feedback. It's the leader's job to create the safe place to make honest feedback acceptable and even desirable.

– Robb LeCount

Chapter Eight

LEADERSHIP LESSON #6:
UNITE TO WIN &
DIVIDE TO CONQUER

Question: Why do big businesses get bigger?

Answer: Because they unite.

Question: Why do small businesses stay small?

Answer: Because they do not know how to unite.

In military school, students are trained to unite to win and divide to conquer. This does not mean one is more important than the other. An officer needs to know when to unite and when to divide. Each action requires a different set of skills. In most military actions, the military needs to unite a large enough force to be able to divide the enemy. That is why the term "Allied Forces" was such an important term during World War II. America had to unite its allies in order to defeat Germany, Japan, and Italy. During the Iraq War, "Coalition Forces" was the term used to unite a multi-national military force against Iraq.

In traditional schools, students are taught to divide to conquer. From day one, students are pitted against each other. Tests are taken as individuals, as the school system looks for smart students and divides or separates them from the weaker students. This process continues until only those the system anoints as the 'smartest,' enter the best schools. Once in the best schools, the process of divide-and-conquer continues.

From day one at the academy, we were trained to unite people. We were taught the ability to unite people was an essential leadership skill. Although we took tests and were graded as we were in traditional schools, tremendous effort was put into our development as leaders, leaders who knew when to unite and when to divide.

From day one at the Academy, we wore the same uniforms and marched in unison. Individual identity was stripped away. We learned to identify ourselves as a group, not as individuals. That is why people in the military tend to identify themselves by their unit, such as Army Ranger, Navy Seal, or Force Recon Marine.

In flight school the process continued, where we wore the same flight suites. The only details that differentiated us were our names, rank, and squadron patches. When we flew, we flew in formation and rarely did we fly as a single aircraft. When we fought, we fought as a team. While strong as individuals, we knew we had more power as a united force, fighting as a team.

A Dog-Eat-Dog World

When most students enter the business world, they enter with the same dog-eat-dog attitude from the world of traditional academics. They compete for jobs just as they competed for grades in school. They want to stand out, rather than stand as a group. In their minds, if they stood out, they had a better chance for promotion and pay raises. Why help your fellow worker get ahead when your fellow worker is your competition?

Look at the CASHFLOW Quadrant pictured below:

Most employees migrate from the E quadrant to the S quadrant. They want to do their own thing. They want to do things their way. They want to stand out. They want to be individuals. Most S-quadrant people remain small, rarely migrating to the B quadrant simply because they know how to divide, but they do not know how to unite.

Uniting people requires leadership skills. Uniting people means asking people to join a larger group, focus on a higher cause, often at the sacrifice of self-interests, self-importance, and self-identity. Getting people to operate as a group at the sacrifice of self-importance is often the toughest job of a leader, especially if the leader needs to be self-important.

Leadership skills are essential for B-quadrant leaders. Specialized skills are essential for S-quadrant leaders. B-quadrant businesses can grow because the business is system-driven, rather than being dependent upon specialized people.

Even as a pilot flying solo, I knew I was not up there on my own. I was flying because I had a large organization behind me.

At the Academy, we were taught to do things the 'Kings Point way.' In the Marine Corps, we were taught to do things the 'Marine Corps way.' Doing things your own way often led to severe disciplinary action. From day one, we were taught to respect the ways of the organization.

As young officers, we were trained to respect precise repetition. Repetition gave power to the organization, especially in combat. For example, when we saluted, we saluted exactly the same way every time. When we flew, we all flew the same way. Precise repetition gives the organization the power to move as an organization. Anyone who wanted to do things their way put the rest of the organization at risk. Individuals were liabilities who could not be trusted to perform with precision, in synch with the rest of the team. If someone had to do things their way, we sent them away. Individuals like that got people killed.

In business, I meet many people who come to work with the "I want to do things my way" attitude. They are disrespectful to the ways of the organization. They are often out of harmony with the rest of organization. They are out of synch.

One of the greatest gifts I received from the Academy and the Marine Corps was the discipline to learn to do things 'their way.' To do that, I had to swallow my pride, my individuality, so I could serve with a higher purpose as part of a much larger team. Today in business, that discipline gives me the unfair advantage over people who want to be stars or prima donnas in business, people who know how to divide but not unite.

Due to my military training, I am much more respectful of organizations and their rituals. For example, when I go into a church, I am mindful of respecting their ways and rituals. To do anything less is extremely disrespectful. I know the importance of rituals and understand that rituals have the power to unite as well as divide. I have noticed that organizations with strong rituals, organizations such as the Catholic Church or the Jewish faith, the Buddhists, and Muslims, have the power to survive for centuries. Companies with strong rituals are stronger than companies without rituals.

In the military, we were trained in the ritual of saluting a higher-ranking officer. Trained to say, "Yes, sir." We were trained to stop and salute the flag during flag-raising ceremonies and when the flag is being taken down. To violate those rituals would demonstrate the highest degree of disrespect for the country we were being trained to serve.

So, when I have someone come to my business and want to do things their way, not respecting the ways and rituals of the business,

I generally let them go on their way. If a person does not understand the importance of respect and respect for rituals, then they probably won't earn my respect or the respect of the team.

As stated earlier, respect binds people together. Disrespect divides and alienates people. Unfortunately, I meet many people who went to school but did not learn the difference between respect and disrespect.

The Power of Connectivity

One of the greatest of all human needs is connectivity. This is why cell phones are such a powerful tool and a great business. The same goes for religions, sports teams, and political parties. This is why businesses want to become brands, brands that connect to and with specific groups of people.

Great leaders have the power to connect people. Great leaders are role models who inspire others to feel they are part of something bigger than themselves. The more connective power the leader has, the more power the group will have. And the more powerful the leader, the more opposition the group will attract. This is why the leader needs to be legally, ethically, and morally strong, aligned to their mission, and in integrity with what they stand for. If the integrity is broken, the connectivity with their group is broken. Look what happened to Bernie Madoff the leader of a $60-billion Ponzi scheme. People who once loved him, trusting him with their life savings, now despise him.

Ironically, integrity is more important in the world of criminals. In other words, if you are going to be a crook, you better be a real crook. In the world of outlaws, there are still laws… their own laws and their own justice, but laws nevertheless.

The military has its own set of rules and regulations. There, as well, rules and regulations both unite and divide. If you follow the rules you are connected; if you break the rules you are divided, separated from the group.

In the military, a higher set of laws is the Code of Honor. A code of honor is a spiritual bond. As Marines, we followed a strict code of honor.

These were some of the points:

1. I will fight and resist capture.

2. If captured, I will give only my name, rank, and serial number.

3. I will not give any information that would be useful to the enemy.

4. I will not desert a fellow combatant in need.

5. I am prepared to give my life so others may live.

In business, I have a personal Code of Honor.

1. I work for my customers and my employees first.

2. The welfare of my empoyees is as important as my welfare.

3. I manage my money responsibly.

4. I acquire assets before I acquire liabilities.

5. I give more if I want more.

A Code of Honor unites people at a spiritual level. Anyone who violates the Code, after agreeing to abide by it, must be dealt with. If the person does not wish to follow the Code, then he or she should leave the organization In this case, the Code of Honor divides people.

ACTION STEPS
Exercises to Develop Your Leadership Skills

1. Discuss the differences between uniting and dividing people.

2. Discuss ways people are united. Discuss ways people are divided.

3. Why is it difficult for people who want to do things 'their way' to become leaders?

4. Discuss the importance of rules, having clear rules, following rules, and bringing justice if rules are broken.

5. What should a leader do if a person does not want to follow the rules of the organization?

6. Why are leaders, rules, and rituals important for B-quadrant businesses?

7. What are some rituals that you follow? What are the rituals of your church, if you attend church? What are your family rituals? How do rituals unite? How do rituals divide?

8. What is connectivity? Name people who have connectivity. Name people who do not.

9. What is a Code of Honor? Why is it a spiritual set of rules?

10. How does a Code of Honor unite? How does it divide?

A Final Word

One of the first objectives of the Academy was to break us of our old habits. They did this through enforced reward or punishment. For example, if a person had a bad habit of being late, the consequences were severe. If the student refused to change this simple habit to being early rather than being late, the student was expelled.

From day one, we were trained to do things the Academy's way… not our way. We were being trained to be leaders, leaders who knew how to unite and how to divide. We were drilled in practicing both skills because both skills have power. I use these same skills in business today. That is why I have a B-quadrant business. That is why The Rich Dad Company is a worldwide brand. The Rich Dad Company unites people who want financial freedom more than they want job security, people who want to be investors rather than gamblers, and to be entrepreneurs instead of employees.

Robb's Report

Earlier in this book, I told you about being tasked with getting my company to follow me in running laps around the base. My first attempt failed as I tried to bribe my company to run with me.

After a small talk from my Company Commander I tried again. I went to each member of my Company and, instead of offering bribes, I offered team… and family. I started my conversation with the fact that I messed up. I made a mistake. I followed that by saying "If you make a mistake I will be there to help carry the burden. I will help you even if you don't help me. What I want is a team. I want us to be united and look out for each other. I will help you. It's up to you whether or not you want to help me."

I was uniting my team. I looked at each individual and tried to put myself in his shoes. What would they want to hear? I knew that deep down I wanted to belong, to a team… to a family. That was really what I was offering to my fellow shipmates. I would be there for you. I was offering unity.

And it worked! Every member of the squad joined me. We faced my punishment together and as a unit. They did not have to endure my pain. They could have left me out there alone. But they didn't. They wanted to feel the bond of a unit and they were willing to make the first sacrifice.

I learned so much that day. I learned the draw and attraction of belonging and the need it fulfills. What I had not learned yet was the power of unity.

That lesson came about five years later. I was stationed in Antarctica. Cold does not describe it. My squadron was very united. We all moved as one. We knew what the others were thinking, always.

Our squadron split into teams and played softball. (A little FYI here: there is no 'soft' in softball when the temperatures are below zero.)

Even when you are united, you still can have a standout player. We had Morrison. This guy could hit, throw, and catch like a pro. The whole squadron was constantly telling him to try out for a professional team as soon as his tour was over. While our team was great and united, we all knew we owed a lot of our success to Morrison.

As you might have expected, our winning streak did not last. Morrison received a 'Dear John' letter and completely fell apart. Our unit was close. We tried to console and comfort Morrison. We tried to take his pain on as a unit. Nothing worked. He went catatonic. The unit stayed close and did all we could do to help. We picked up the slack in his work as a mechanic. We worked with him and checked his work when he was done. The extra work sucked, but being a unified team is awesome and worth it.

On the softball field Morrison was not focused. As a team, we were completely out of sync. We suddenly did not function. As Navy mechanics, we had a number of other mechanics who could pick up the slack. On a softball field everyone has their own duties and responsibilities. When one team member breaks the unity, the whole thing breaks. All of us had our focus in the wrong place and none of us could backup Morrison's errors on the field or at bat.

We started losing. We bonded together. Regained our focus… all of us, except Morrison. We still kept losing. Then Morrison started playing better. He channeled his anger and hurt to his bat and began hitting like never before! But his defense was still not in sync with our team. His throws were too hard, his play too aggressive. We were not united. And we kept losing.

It did not take long for our maintenance chief to notice Morrison's situation. Despite our best efforts to protect Morrison, when a united group fractures it is very obvious to anyone who's watching. Morrison got shipped off to receive help. Our unit knit back together and we began to win again. Turned out we weren't winning due to Morrison. The united team won all of our games without him. We were winning… but it wasn't the same.

This is actually a painful story. While the lesson is that unity wins and division conquers, the more important lesson, to me, is protecting that unity. Do not take it for granted. I often wonder how we could have protected Morrison. I will never take unity for granted again though. I strive for unity in my family and my workplace. It's the most important part of winning.

– Robb LeCount

Chapter Nine

LEADERSHIP LESSON #7: LEADERS ARE TEACHERS

Think of a teacher you loved. What did that teacher do? Did they inspire you? Did they respect you? Did they bring out the best in you?

Who were the teachers who inspired you to be a great student?

Think of a teacher you hated. What caused your lack of respect for that teacher? What did this teacher do? What *didn't* they do?

Remembering Your Worst Teachers

For a teacher to be a great teacher, they must be a great leader. They must be someone the student looks up to. It is difficult to learn from someone you do not respect.

In traditional schools there are great teachers and bad teachers. In military schools, there are also great teachers and bad teachers. The difference is that bad teachers in traditional schools can cost you bad grades. Bad teachers in the military can cost you your life.

In both traditional and military schools, I had bad grades because I was a bad student. I had horrible grades because, in my opinion, I had horrible teachers. They didn't inspire me. They didn't make me hungry to learn.

The best teachers I had were individuals I looked up to. The worst teachers were teachers who had not earned my respect. My grades reflected my level of respect for them—or lack of it.

My favorite instructor at the Academy was my English professor. He was a West Point, U.S. Military Academy-graduate, and a B-17 pilot in World War II. He was shot down over France and escaped to fly again. He inspired me to become a pilot.

In 1969 I graduated from the Academy and was hired by Standard Oil of California. I had achieved the American Dream: a college graduate, a high-paying job with a giant corporation, working for seven months on and five months off, a long paid vacation.

At the same time Naval Academy graduates were earning approximately, $2,400 a year. A few of my fellow Merchant Marine Academy graduates were earning over $100,000 a year, the highest paid graduates in the world. I earned less, only $47,000 a year, which wasn't bad pay for a 21-year-old in 1969. I estimate that $47,000 in 1969 would be like earning $200,000 today.

My classmates who were earning over a $100,000 year in 1969 had joined the International Organization of Master, Mates & Pilots, a labor union for ships officers, and were sailing in the war zone. In the Merchant Marine, your pay almost doubles anytime you are in a war zone.

If you saw the movie Captain Phillips, staring Tom Hanks, you know it is the story of a merchant ship taken over by Somali pirates. The civilians on board that ship were being paid war zone pay. Their paychecks were much more generous than the Navy Seals who parachuted in, killed the pirates, and rescued Captain Phillips.

I earned less because I worked for Standard Oil and because I did not join the union. If I had joined the union, Standard Oil would not have hired me. I was sailing between California and Hawaii, Tahiti, and Alaska—hardly a war zone.

I was also draft-exempt, classified "Non-defense vital industry," the vital industry being oil.

Although it seemed that I "had it all," at age 22, the stories from my English teacher haunted me. In my soul, I wanted to fly in combat. And, although draft exempt, my conscience haunted me. I knew it was my duty to serve my country. Four of my uncles served in World War II. One of them was one of two Japanese-Americans captured, and was held as a POW of the Japanese. The more soul searching I did the less important my job, the paycheck, and vacations became.

I had first gone to Vietnam in 1966. I was 19 years old, a midshipman from the Academy, a student on board a freighter carrying bombs to the war zone.

The war did not make sense to me in 1966. At the Academy, we learned the Vietnamese had been at war for over a thousand years, fighting intruders like China and France. The United States was but one more country for them to fight. I was troubled about the war in 1966. I wondered why we were there. And even years later, the war made no sense to me.

After sailing for Standard Oil for only a few months, my conscience finally got the better of me. In late 1969, I resigned from Standard Oil, and reported for U.S. Navy flight school. Starting pay was $2,400 a year. Just the thought of giving up $4,000 a month with five months paid vacation to earn $200 a month (with only two weeks vacation) was a shock to my system. The reality was even worse and it took some adjusting. My friends and family thought I had lost it. But, looking back, I know it was one of the best decisions of my life. I doubt I would have become an entrepreneur if I had stayed with Standard Oil, working for job security, a steady paycheck, paid vacations, benefits, and a cushy retirement.

Today, I meet many "civilians",—corporate warriors who are smart, well-educated, hard workers—but it always seems to me that they lack something. Many want to be entrepreneurs, want start their own business, working for financial freedom rather than job security, but something is missing. They lack that core strength of character, the unstoppable entrepreneurial spirit required for success as an entrepreneur.

One of the first things I noticed in the Marine Corps, was the level of personal responsibility required of each young Marine. Even if the Marine was an 18-year-old private with only a high school education, they had responsibilities few civilians would ever be required to shoulder. For example, on our helicopter gunship in Vietnam, a young corporal had to know how to fix the aircraft as

well as fire machine guns and rockets in combat. If someone was
wounded, they could double as a corpsman, saving lives in the field.

On our gunships, there was a crew of five—two pilots, two
gunners, and a crew chief. On our aircraft, there was no such thing
as rank. There is only respect and responsibility. Each one of us was
a leader on the same team. If each of us did our job, we lived. If I
pulled rank to get someone to do something, we died.

Flying in Vietnam, gave me the courage to become an entrepreneur.

Today, I meet many people who want to become entrepreneurs,
but they lack the core strengths that the military instills in young
people. Most lack the discipline, people skills, and leadership
experience to take the leap of faith—to leave job security and a steady
paycheck—and become an entrepreneur.

Two Types of Pain

One of the more important lessons I learned at the Academy and
in the Marine Corps was the lesson on two types of pain. They are:

1. The Pain of Discipline.

2. The Pain of Regret.

There are life-changing differences between these two types of
pain. The pain of discipline is temporary, short-lived. The pain of
regret is eternal.

For example, I rarely want to go the gym. I would rather sit on
a couch and watch TV. Yet I know that I will feel terrible longer if I
don't go to the gym. It is the pain of discipline, the 20-minute Rule
that gets me off the couch, even if I don't feel like exercising.

What is the 20-minute Rule? It's the motivation I use to get me to
do anything I do not want to do… like go to the gym. I know, that
I'll feel pain for 20-minutes or so, but after 20-minutes I am generally
happy doing what I did not want to do.

Most people are not willing to go through those 20 minutes
of pain. Instead, they live a life of regret, which can be eternal.

When I meet unhappy, unsuccessful, unhealthy, unwealthy, and unfulfilled people, I believe their pain is the pain of regret. They lack the discipline to push through their pain, doing what they need to do, to get to the other side of their pain. Rather than doing what they do not want to do, but know they need to do, many trade the short-term pain of discipline for the long-term pain of regret. Rather than go through their pain now, many want the easy answer, the magic pill, and the pain-free formula that will get them to the next level of life.

Many who want to get rich without pain tend to go to Las Vegas or play the lottery, living with the illusion that they'll strike it rich.

The Pain of Pain

There is a lot of truth to the saying, "No pain no gain." I will always be grateful to the Academy and the Marine Corps for instilling in me the discipline to push through my pain. As you know by now, I was an average, lazy, student much of my life. I studied just enough to pass the tests. Going to the Academy and flying for the Marine Corps changed my lazy ways.

A proud mother of a new Marine once wrote:

"For all of those that have son's or daughter's at boot camp let me pass on what I found. Let me give you a little background first.

"When my son left home he had no motivation, he was lazy, slobby, no pride, no self worth. This is the boy that got off the bus March 18th at Parris Island.

"The man that I met on Thursday for Parents Day is AWESOME. There is no way I can describe to you all the difference. He looks different, he walks different, he talks different, he has such a sense of bearing and pride all I could do was look at him in awe.

"Oh yes, the training is hard, what he went through is unimaginable to any one that has not been there. They are definitely taught to be Warriors. Let me tell you the surprise of what else they are taught. My Marine son has better values, better morals, better manners than any

one I know. It is so much more than 'Yes, Sir... Yes, Ma'am'...
so much more.

"He cares about how he looks, he cares about what he does, and it's
not a boastful, bad-ass thing. He is a true gentleman. I saw patience,
and a calmness in him that I have never seen. I could never express my
gratitude enough to the Marine Corps for what they have given my son."

"Cybil"
Mother of a Marine

The discipline of the Marine Corps and the leadership training from my instructors and commanding officers taught me the value of the pain of discipline. I am alive today because I learned the value of going through the pain of discipline.

As I've said, Lt Ted Greene and I crashed our Huey in the ocean off of Vietnam. Our engine quit and our crew of five swam for over four hours. In the photo below, you see what a Huey gunship looks like as it hits the water.

In another incident, Lt Joe Ezell and I went down due to a dual hydraulic failure. As far as we know, we are the only pilots and crew to survive such an equipment failure. Hueys do not fly without hydraulics.

Without having endured the earlier pain of discipline, we would be dead.

If any one of us had died, those who survived would have had to live with the pain of regret.

Every time we flew, we "practiced" facing death every day, on every mission. We never took a break from the pain of discipline, the practice of facing death. When our engine quit and when the hydraulic systems failed, everyone on board—from crew to pilots, officers and enlisted men—operated as a highly efficient, disciplined team, functioning under extreme pressure, facing fears few will ever face.

The discipline of facing my fears, the discipline of doing what I need to do even if I do not want to do it, has made me a pretty good entrepreneur. Everyday, as an entrepreneur, I face my fears. Entrepreneurs cannot count on a steady paycheck or a big corporation to protect them from the real world of business and its challenges.

When people say, "Do what you love and the money will follow," I say, "BS. In business, a person must do what they know they must, even if they hate doing it."

My roommate on board the carrier was 1Lt Jack Bergman, who became LtGen Jack Bergman. Jack was a pilot of a CH-46 in Vietnam. He had a crew of five. As a LtGen, he had over 200,000 men and women under his command. The lessons in leadership learned with a crew of five grew into the ability to be a leader of hundreds of thousands.

Jack not only became a General in the Marine Corps—he was also an airline captain, flying for Northwest Airlines, and an entrepreneur in the medical equipment field.

Jack and I spent hours on board the carrier, discussing the war, military tactics, and leadership styles. Although we did not always agree, I have carried many of the lessons he taught me into business and life.

These Marines used their flight skills and experience in civilian life: 1Lt Joe Ezell became a captain who flew for Emery Air, 1Lt Ted Greene became a captain flying for United Airlines, and as I've stated, Jack Bergman flew as a captain for Northwest Airlines while still flying for the Marine Corps. If you understand the airline industry, you know how difficult it is for a helicopter pilot to land a job flying for a commercial airline. I believe it was the discipline learned in the Marine Corps that led to their leadership and success in the civilian world.

We all served together in Marine squadron HMM-164. Due to the leadership of our commanding officer Lt Colonel Hertberg and executive officer Major Moore the squadron was awarded both the NUC, the Navy Unit Citation, and a MUC, Meritorious Unit Citation.

I mention these Unit Citations because there is distinct difference between medals, such as the Medal of Honor or Silver Star, which are awarded to individuals, versus, Unit Citations, which recognize and commend an entire squadron. Unit Citations speak to the quality of leadership of our unit leaders. Our squadron was not recognized for how many people we killed, but for how well we performed in combat and how many men came home alive.

I believe the reason 1Lt Bergman, Greene, Ezell, and I went on to become successful in life, after leaving HMM 164, was due, in large part, to the lessons learned from our squadron's leaders. True leaders inspire others to be great leaders.

Of all my lessons in leadership, my best lesson came from the young corporal, my door gunner, who had just received word that he was a new father. I wrote about him in an early chapter of this book. In many ways, he was my very best teacher.

I asked him, "Is it OK with you if your son grows up without a father?" And, without hesitation, he said, "Yes, sir. It's OK with me. I'm ready to go." He then smiled, assuring me really was "ready to go"—ready to die, if necessary—by saying, "Lieutenant, you do your job and I'll do mine."

Quitting my high-paying job seemed easy after what that young man was willing to sacrifice.

In retrospect, my decision to quit my job with Standard Oil to serve my country transformed me from a money-driven, high-paid employee to a mission-driven entrepreneur.

As General George Patton said:

"The coward is the one who lets his fear overcome his sense of duty."

Two Eyes, Two Ears... One Mouth

Looking at the illustration of a human face pictured below, you'll notice that it has two eyes, two ears, and one mouth. This means we learn best by watching and listening, and less by talking.

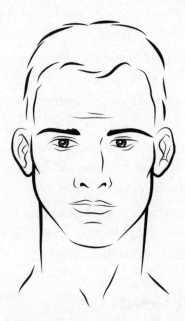

Unfortunately, many teachers think that by talking more, their students learn more.

Great leaders and teachers are often people of few words. Bad leaders and teachers often talk a lot. They give orders that no one follows. They often share wisdom no one wants. Bad teachers and leaders often try to threaten you into listening to them. Others try to get you to like them. Some are sweet, complimentary, but often phony. Both fear and politeness are masks for deeper insecurities.

We have all heard the term "the strong, silent type." The teachers and leaders I respected most were the strong, silent type. They were men and women of few words... but when they spoke, people listened.

The Person Who Asks the Questions Is in Control

When a person talks too much, they are failing to learn by observing and by listening. Great leaders and teachers, listen and observe more than they talk.

When they talk, they tend to ask questions because questions give them an opportunity to watch, listen, and learn more. That is why in a courtroom, attorneys ask questions. If the defendant asks a question, the attorney will snap back saying, "I ask the questions here." Attorneys know that the person who asks the questions is in control.

In business my rich dad taught me to be interested... not interesting. He said, "People who try to be interesting are often boring. People who are interested control the conversation, learn more, and do not have to do all the talking."

In sales, I found that if I was interested, asked questions, listened with my ears, observed with my eyes, and let the customer do most of the talking, I made more money.

When teaching a class, I do my best to have my students talk more than I talk. I have noticed that the more they talk and discuss—and the less I talk—the more the students learn.

Changing Habits Changes Lives

Military schools focus on changing bad habits and replacing them with better habits. To achieve this, the academies focus on developing the students mentally, emotionally, physically, and spiritually. A student who could not change the many facets of their habit patterns was often expelled.

Traditional schools focus primarily on the student's mind. Personal behavior was not important, as long as they achieved the desired grades.

Habits are the difference between rich, middle class, and poor people. A poor person cannot become a middle class person until they change their habits. Changing habits requires making changes mentally, emotionally, physically, and spiritually. The same is true for middle class people who want to become rich.

Money alone does not change habits. That is why so many lottery winners and sports stars, people who come from poor backgrounds, return to being poor, once the money is gone.

The reason I created the *CASHFLOW* board game is because games are great teaching tools. Games have the power to change a person's habits by engaging them mentally, emotionally, physically, and spiritually.

Reading books and listening to lectures alone will not change habits. Just as reading books and listening to lectures, alone, would not turn me into a pilot. I could know all the right answers in the classroom, but I still have to fly the plane. The same is true with becoming a rich person.

The Cone of Learning

Cone of Learning		
After 2 weeks we tend to remember		**Nature of Involvement**
90% of what we say and do	Doing the Real Thing	**Active**
	Simulating the Real Experience	
	Doing a Dramatic Presentation	
70% of what we say	Giving a Talk	
	Participating in a Discussion	
50% of what we hear and see	Seeing it Done on Location	**Passive**
	Watching a Demonstration	
	Looking at an Exhibit Watching a Demonstration	
	Watching a Movie	
30% of what we see	Looking at Pictures	
20% of what we hear	Hearing Words (Lecture)	
10% of what we read	Reading	

Source: Cone of Learning adapted from Dale, (1969)

You may notice, in studying the Cone of Learning pictured on the previous page, that reading and listening to lectures are the least effective way to learn. Yet, this is the focus of the education system and process in traditional schools. This is how traditional schools measure intelligence.

At the top of the Cone of Learning are 'simulations' and 'doing the real thing.' Military schools focus a lot on simulations and doing the real thing.

To make matters worse, traditional education punishes students who make mistakes. By using simulations and live exercises, military teachers encourage students to make mistakes and learn from them.

At the Academy, I spent many hours sailing sailboats and steering powered ships. In flight school, I spent hours flying simulators on the ground and even more hours flying real planes. I loved learning in a military environment because their method of education engaged me mentally, emotionally, physically, and spiritually.

When I decided to teach others the same lessons my rich dad taught me, I knew the second best way to teach was to use a game. That is why Kim and I created the *CASHFLOW* board game. We believed that it was best to learn by playing with play money before putting real money at risk.

When you look at the financial statement from the *CASHFLOW* board game, it is easy to understand why the rich get richer.

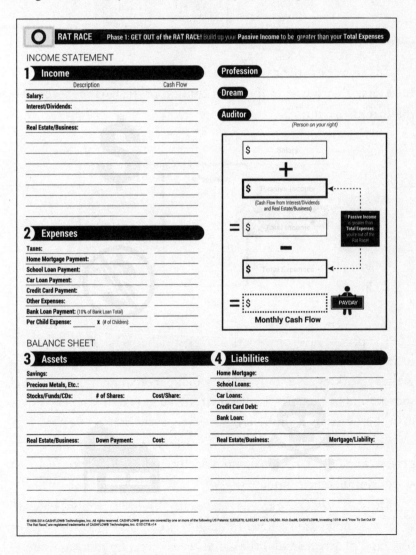

Most students go to school to learn to be Es and Ss... Employees or Specialists. They leave school and focus on the Income Statement.

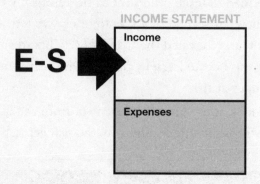

The rich teach their kids to be Bs and Is, big-Business owners or Investors. They focus on the Asset column of the balance sheet, versus the Income column.

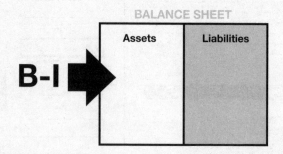

The primary reason why the rich get richer is because they focus on acquiring assets, assets that put money in their pockets without working. Not only do they make more money every year, if successful, but they pay a lower percentage in taxes than people who earn their income from their labor via a paycheck.

The power of the *CASHFLOW* game is its ability to train a person, mentally, emotionally, physically, and spiritually to focus on assets, not income from labor.

The *CASHFLOW* game is the teacher. The game allows people to teach people. This teacher never gets tired. As long as the students play (and play repeatedly) the game keeps revealing more and more lessons. The more mistakes the students make, with play money, the smarter they get with their real money.

Every year, Kim and I focus on how many more assets we will acquire. That is why we continue to get richer. We do not focus on working harder for money. We do not go back to school to learn ways to earn more money. We work harder to create, acquire, or improve our assets. That is why we created the *CASHFLOW* games— *CASHFLOW 101*, *CASHFLOW 202*, and *CASHFLOW for Kids*—as both board games, electronic versions and social-mobile games. The *CASHFLOW* games are simulations of what we do in real life.

ACTION STEPS
Exercises to Develop Your Leadership Skills

1. Who were your best teachers? What did they do to inspire you to learn?

2. Who were your worst teachers? What made them ineffective and terrible?

3. In conversations, how often are you talking? What percentage of the time are you talking? What percentage of the time are you watching and listening? The next time you have a conversation with a person, count the number of questions you ask. Notice how many the other person asks. Then determine who learned more about the other.

4. Study the Cone of Learning. What are the differences between learning from books and lectures versus simulations and doing the real thing?

5. How can a person learn if, emotionally, they are trained to be afraid of making mistakes?

6. Why do games engage a person mentally, emotionally, physically, and spiritually?

7. What are the differences between a person who focuses on going to school to learn to work for money and a person who focuses on acquiring assets?

8. Why does one person work harder and why does another person get richer without working harder?

9. Why does money alone not make you rich? Why does giving people money not solve their money problems?

10. Why do leaders have to be teachers?

A Final Word

The motto of the U.S. Merchant Marine Academy is 'Acta Non Verba,' *Deeds Not Words*. As a person who is very shy (basically pretty quiet, and dull at parties) I found the Academy's motto to be especially beneficial in my life. Rather than attempt to be a great talker, I decided it best to let my actions do my talking for me. Today, rather than talk about doing things, I'd rather keep quiet and do them. The more I accomplish in my life the less I have to say… to be heard.

Robb's Report

I was a child with no boundaries. I did not know it at the time, but I desperately wanted boundaries. Of course I wasn't going to make it easy for anyone who tried. I required a special kind of teacher. I had rejected the teachers at school. I did not listen to my mother.

I needed a teacher who was a leader first.

I've written about a few of my great leaders. Each of them was a great teacher. Great leaders and teachers are often people of few words. They listen more than they talk. Nelson Mandela said he learned about leadership from his father, a chieftain.

Mandela's father told him that the key to being a great leader was to talk last. He said that it is much wiser to listen to many thoughts and opinions rather than tell people what to think. When he would have his tribe meetings he would place his advisors in a circle and ask questions. Then he would listen. Listen to all the wisdom in the room. He would then ask more questions and listen. Finally he would speak. Leaders talk last.

This was how my Company Commander, the man who taught

would come into the barracks and ask questions. Very rarely did he make statements. He did not threaten us into listening to him. He watched more than he spoke. He communicated far more with his actions, and the time he took the time to observe spoke more loudly than his words.

Chief Burk, the one who made me run laps around the base and who first saw my leadership potential, had a genius for teaching through actions.

Although he wanted me to lead, he never told me how to do it. Instead he just sent me in to learn through my actions… and my failures. Then he would ask me a whole lot of questions until an idea, a plan of action, occurred to me. Then he'd send me out to take action again. I don't think I ever learned as much as I did through that man's leadership.

The Navy gave me LOTS to read. And the Navy gave us a lot of lectures. But the things I learned the most from were the experiences my CC gave me. It's like Robert says: You learn more from doing and simulation than from reading and lecture.

When I was given a section to be in charge of I wanted to lead them the same way my CC led me. I wanted to be a great leader and have the best section. I held tons of meetings. I assigned tons of reading. I gave quizzes. My section was going to be the best! Until we weren't.

I did not understand. How could I have failed? What was wrong with my section? I did everything right. My section stunk!

The next day I was called into my CC's office to review the results of my section. I was humiliated and ashamed. My CC read the review silently and then looked up.

"What do you think about the results?" he asked.

"I think they're horrible."

"What is your plan to improve them?"

"I guess I'll make them study harder and longer. I guess I was too easy on them." Then, I whispered, "… and get a smarter section."

That was what he was waiting for.

"I don't think it's your section. Is it possible it's your leadership and teaching style?"

"What?!?" I was incredulous. "I did it just like you…" then I realized what had prompted his questions.

My CC did not teach through lecture and reading. He always taught through questions and action assignments. He was doing it right now.

It made sense.

"Permission to be excused?" I knew what I needed to do.

Leadership isn't showing the team how smart you are and that you deserve the position. I realized that I needed to be a teacher.

After that day I led my team just as I had been led. We still read in books, but then we practiced on actual tasks. While the team practiced, I asked questions. There were times I didn't even know all the answers. I think I ended up learning just as much, if not more, than my section.

And yes. Our scores greatly improved.

– Robb LeCount

Chapter Ten
LEADERSHIP LESSON #8:
LEADERSHIP IS ONE BIG SALES JOB

Leaders who have changed the world have been the greatest salespeople in the world. Jesus Christ, Buddha, and Mohammed are among the greatest religious leaders in the world. To get human beings to follow a righteous path, rather than a life of sex, cheating, thieving, and lying, they had to be the best salesmen in the world.

Barack Obama beat Senator John McCain in the 2008 race for U.S. Presidency because Obama was a better salesman with a better sales team behind him. Obama is the first person to win the U.S. Presidency using the Internet. He outpaced Mitt Romney in 2012 to secure a second term.

In business, the business leaders are sales leaders. If they stop being sales leaders, they stop being business leaders. In life, rich people have more to sell than poor people. Those who sell the most, become leaders in their fields. Simply put, leadership is about sales... and sales is about leadership.

My fist leadership task at the Academy was getting my section mates, my own classmates, to follow my orders. I distinctly remember my first time as section leader. I remember being nervous as I said, "Section, atten—hut."

Immediately, one of my section mates said, "Screw you, Kiyosaki." I repeated the command and got the same response.

I said it again, and this time I got an "F... you!"

Getting angry, I finally I found some courage and snarled, "Look, Murphy, if you screw with me, I'll screw with you when you're section leader." Laughing, Murphy said, "I was wondering when you were going to grow some balls. For awhile, you sounded like my little sister."

With that I bit my tongue, resisting the urge to respond to Murphy's remarks, and reissued my command, "Atten—shun," with much more authority. Immediately, the entire section snapped to attention. No more wise cracks. "Right face" was my next command and to my surprised, they all turned on command. With, "Forward... march" my section of about 20 teenagers was finally on its way, marching to class.

That day, I learned my first lesson in leadership. Leadership is more than just saying the right words... just giving orders. It's about earning the respect of those you will lead. Just because you're in charge, does not mean people will listen. Leadership is a sales job. People do not just blindly follow someone who proclaims themselves their 'leader.' People want to be led. But they also want someone they can look up to. People want someone they can respect.

In the military, leaders ask their troops to be willing to give their lives. In business, leaders ask their customers to give their money. In either case, leaders must sell.

Three Parts to Communication

There are three elements that make up communication. They are:

1. Words = 7%

2. Tone | Timber | Tempo = 34%

3. Physical Appearance and Presence = 55%

Obviously the percentages cited above are approximations, based on everyday communication. The reason the percentages do not add up to 100% is to allow for other factors. These percentages will vary, based upon the person and the environment. The point is that communication is more than just words. Silence is often the most powerful of all communications.

Words

The percentages illustrate the point: Words are the least important aspect of communication. This is why so many people say, "I told him what to do, but he didn't do it." or "I said all the right words." Words play only a small role in powerful and success communication.

This does not mean words are not important. Words can be very important. But in the context of everyday speech, it is the following two parts of communication that affect the power of words.

Tone | Timber | Tempo

Tone refers to emotional tone of the voice. Someone who is angry will get more attention than someone who is wimpy. Good speakers use varying emotional tones when they speak. People who speak in a monotone, are often boring.

Timber refers to the quality of a person's voice. For example, someone with a squeak, raspy, or nasal voice will have more difficulty communicating. Many people earn a respectable living doing radio spots, simply because the timber of their voice is soothing, strong, and inspires trust.

Many of us have heard a person who uses all the right words, but sounds insincere. This is often a case of emotional tone and timber not matching the words. For example a person who says "I said, 'I'm sorry.'" in an angry tone and harsh timber, may communicate a meaning exactly opposite of "I'm sorry."

Tempo is the pace of speech. In the United States, people in the North tend to speak faster than people from the South. If a person speaks more slowly than the tempo the audience is accustomed to, sales are lost.

To be an effective leader, the leader must be aware of their tone, tempo, and timber as they speak.

Physical Appearance and Presence:

Most of us have seen people who are so beautiful that they take your breath away. You do not care what they say. In other words, how you look or gestures you make are the most powerful part of a leader's communication.

A silent smile can communicate much more than words. So, too, can a silent frown communicate loudly. Showing someone the middle finger has provoked more fights than words.

Most speakers stand behind a podium and lecture. This robs them of their most powerful communication tool and limits the effectiveness of their message. Standing in front of the country's flag may inspire people who are patriotic. Walking on stage accompanied by guards armed with rifles may make it easier for a dictator to make his or her point.

The reason television has been such a powerful medium is because it communicates visually. Visual communication is more powerful than auditory communication alone. A fat person selling a weight control program will have a harder time selling than a thin person. A person dressed like a bum selling financial success might find few takers of his or her product. Appearance communicates health, wealth, and attractiveness. Many people think their clothes and grooming do not matter. If you believe that, then go to work naked. See what happens…

Personal appearance was a very big subject at the Academy and in the Marine Corps. It was important that we felt proud to wear our uniforms. That is why uniforms are uniforms. Uniforms unite. Although our uniforms were the same, it was important to display rank or rate. We knew the difference between silver stars, for generals, and gold bars for 2nd lieutenants. Uniforms also communicated to others your specialty. For example, pilots wore wings and submariners wore dolphins. In the Army, a green beret was a badge of honor.

When I do public appearances, I take the time to make sure my appearance speaks before I do. I dress with an edge. Also, I do not choose my clothes. I have no taste. I let professional dressers choose my clothes. I say nothing, pay the bill, and wear the clothes.

True Communication Is the Response You Get

Most of us have gone to a class or lecture and fallen asleep. The speaker was boring. The speaker may have been intelligent, well dressed, and you may have had an interest in their subject… but the response the speaker got was… snoring.

A good guide to developing your leadership and sales skills is "True communication is the response you get." In other words, it's not what you say. It is the feedback you get that is your measure of success or failure.

In sales, if you have done a great job, sales will go up. Money is your response. If you do a bad job, people shake your hand, and say, "I'll think about it." In this case, 'no money' is your response. Lack of interest was your communication or feedback. You were probably boring and wasted their time—and your time. You need to take the feedback, the response, and learn from it. Practice to your presentations and your pitch until you get the response you want.

Responsibility is made up of two words. Response and ability… the ability to get the response you want. That is leadership. That is also salesmanship. Poor leaders blame their workers. Poor salespeople blame the customer. That is not responsibility. That is blame, and I see blame as standing for be-lame. People who blame will not develop into leaders. Leaders are people who invest the time to develop the ability to get the response they want.

Sales… the #1 Skill of an Entrepreneur

In 1974, I left the Marine Corps. Rather than follow my poor dad's advice (to get a job as an airline pilot, or go back to sea as ships officer, or go back to school and get my Masters degree and work for the government) I decided to follow my rich dad's path and become an entrepreneur.

"If you are going to be an entrepreneur, selling is your most important skill," he told me. Those were the words of advice from my rich dad that have stayed with me as I've traveled my entrepreneurial path.

In 1974, I joined the Xerox Corporation because they had a great sales training program. Once the sales training program was over, I hit the streets of Honolulu and immediately failed as a salesman. I was horrible at sales. I wanted to quit every Monday.

Rich dad's advice was to "Fail faster." He said, "How can you learn to sell by making only two or three sales calls a day?" Taking his advice, I would leave Xerox at 5 p.m. and go to the offices of a non-profit organization, to "dial for dollars" for free—and make more 'sales calls' every day. My goal was to make at least 30 phone calls between 6 and 9 p.m. each day. Although I did not do that well dialing for dollars, my sales numbers at Xerox started improving. By the time I left Xerox in 1978 to start my first entrepreneurial business, my nylon and Velcro surfer wallet business, I was number one in sales for Xerox in Honolulu.

In 1984, I decided to teach. Once again, I followed the same process. I began speaking for free to anyone who would listen. I did previews, selling seminars for free—just for the experience. I had friends like Blair Singer who would lock me in a room to practice, two to three nights a week. Blair was ruthless. He demanded I become better and better as a speaker from stage. Soon I was being asked to speak all over the world. And, again, I worked for free, asking only for transportation and expenses. By 1986, Kim and I were being paid as speakers, simply because there was so much demand for what we were teaching. We were finally getting the response we wanted. And by 1994, Kim and I were financially free.

Today, Kim and I travel the world as teachers and leaders in the field of financial education. Today, Blair is a leading authority on sales and sales training. His programs are tough and life changing. He has the power to bring out the sales leader in people.

My advice to people who want to be leaders is, "Keep practicing, keep taking feedback, keep improving, until you have the ability to get the response you want. That is response-ability. That is the essence of leadership."

All Decisions Are Emotional

Dealing with people who are like you is relatively easy. Dealing with people who are different—lazy, belligerent, sloppy, or incompetent—requires tremendous skill. To be able to change a person's point of view requires more than words.

Standing your ground and having courage to defend your views, especially if they're unpopular, takes more than words. It takes courage. True communication involves risks, as the diagram below will explain. It takes risk because all decisions are emotional.

The diagram is a simple triangle diagram of a human being.

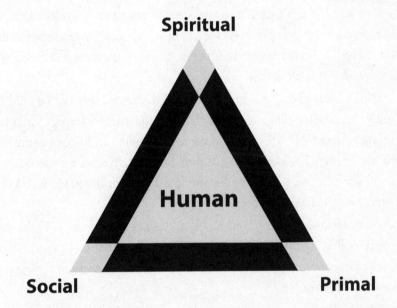

Leaders and sales people are ineffective if they do not penetrate the social façade all of us have. To be effective, the leader or sales person must get through to the person at a primal level. Remember, humans are not rational. They are very emotional and all decisions are affected by emotions. If a person does not get past the social veneer, nothing happens. That is why when advertising to young men, advertisers use good-looking women. When advertising to older men, good-looking women are used. Because sex is primal.

When selling cars, advertisers sell family safety when selling Volvos. Safety is primal. Ferrari uses sex. Again, sex is primal. Magazine or television ads that do not hit a primal chord meet with less success (read: fewer sales) than ads that do.

Fear, Sex, Desire, Love, Respect, Ruggedness, and Attractiveness are a few primal 'hot buttons' that leaders and sales people must hit. Remember: All decisions are emotional. If it's not emotional, it's boring. Boring people are generally poor leaders and poor sales people.

Some of the best sales people I have met are people who put themselves through college by selling products door-to-door and Mormon Missionaries.

Getting through a person's social veneer requires tremendous skill, patience, courage, and perseverance, all of which develop character and self-esteem. Character is not the absence of fear. Character is defined by your actions, in spite of fear.

When I was deciding which branch of the armed services I would fly for, it was a Marine officer's speech that had the greatest impact. Standing on stage, impeccably dressed in Marine Corps blues in front of about 500 young men, he spoke with a strong, authoritative voice and said, "If you want to save people, fly for the Coast Guard. If you want to kill people, join the Marine Corps."

Now, I know this may sound sick to many of you. I know I take great risks sharing my deep, dark, primal side. Yet, that is the truth. That was the presentation that influenced—MADE—my decision. It was not a rational decision.

My family is from the Samurai class of Japan. In World War II, I had seven uncles go to war, five fought against the Germans and Italians and two against the Japanese, with one uncle captured by the Japanese. Fighting is in my blood. When the recruiter said those words, his words struck a chord, bringing to the surface generations of family heritage. His words gave me the courage to fight for my country, at a time when my peers were burning their draft cards, seeking college deferments, running to Canada, and spitting on those who went to war. His words pushed me beyond my fears. His words inspired me to take a stand, to make an irrational decision, a decision that changed the direction of my life.

If you have seen the movie *Born on the Fourth of July* starring Tom Cruise, you may recall a scene very similar to the one I just described. In the movie, the Marine recruiter said almost exactly the same words that my recruiter said to me.

It is true. The Marines are looking for a few good men. That day, in an auditorium filled with about 500 young men, only 25 went to see the Marine recruiter. The rest went to talk to the Navy, Army, Air Force, and Coast Guard recruiters.

ACTION STEPS

Exercises to Develop Your Leadership Skills

1. Discuss the differences between speaking and selling.

2. Why do some people speak... and no one listens?

3. Discuss the three parts of communication: words, tone, and physical appearance and presence.

4. How are tone, timber, and tempo important? What happens if someone speaks with anger? Sadness? Fear? Joy? What happens if the timber of someone's voice is disturbing? What happens if the person speaks too slowly... or too fast?

5. How is physical appearance important? How does your physical appearance 'sell' even before you do?

6. What is the difference between your social side and your primal side?

7. Why are most decisions irrational?

8. How do leaders reach a person's primal side? What skills do they possess that most people do not?

A Final Word

Some people are born leaders. I was not. At the Academy, it was obvious who the natural leaders were. Rather than feel bad about myself, I decided to work on my leadership skills. Today, I continue to work on those skills.

The basis of leadership is courage. The word courage comes from the French word, *la coeur*, which means *the heart*. Courage is not necessary when times are normal. Courage is required when facing any challenge. To develop my leadership skills, I made it a habit to constantly put myself in situations where my courage would be tested. It is a habit I developed at the Academy, in the Marine Corps, and as an entrepreneur. This habit, not my brains, personality, or talents, has been the secret to my success.

As my rich dad said, "I am rich because I do things most people will not do. Success requires sacrifice and I am willing to make those sacrifices." As a military officer, being willing to sacrifice my life was easy. Asking young men, some with families, to sacrifice their lives was hard. Asking young men with families to give their life for their country was the hardest of all my sales jobs. Once I was willing to give my life and ask others to give their lives for their country, becoming an entrepreneur was easy. After all, entrepreneurial business is only the second most hostile environment created by man.

Robb's Report

Robert holds weekly meetings with the staff at Rich Dad. They are the same meetings we record and broadcast for our Insiders subscribers. In one of those meeting he stated that everyone is selling—all the time. There is always someone selling and someone buying. I never thought of it that way before.

When I asked a girl on a date I was selling myself. If she rejected me, then she did not buy. If I stopped pursuing then I am no longer the buyer and she turns into the seller. I bought that she's truly not interested and that it's not worth my time.

Another thing Robert once said is that if he were stranded on an island with a few people, the number one skill he would want in someone is sales. That way he could get whatever he needed—or needed to be done—by selling the stranded group's skills, leveraging those skills and talents to keep them all alive.

Oddly enough, that made a lot of sense. Leadership is just one big sales job. My leaders in the military first had to sell me—make me believe—that they were worthy of my respect. They were selling the fact that they were leaders.

When I first got in trouble with my CC, he started selling me the idea that I was better than the behavior I displayed. He then sold me on the idea that I could be a leader.

Over the years here at Rich Dad I've heard Robert say numerous times that a leader's number one job is to create more leaders. It makes sense. It takes the number one skill, selling, to fulfill the number one job.

When Shane Caniglia, our president here at Rich Dad and a serial entrepreneur, first came to Rich Dad he patiently sold us on his authority. After the team bought into Shane's leadership, he did not hold it tightly in his possession. Instead he began to identify, create, and teach leaders. He created a core team of leaders that carried much of the leadership burden.

As I've written about in previous lessons, unity is not something to take for granted. It has to be worked on and focused on constantly. Shane's main job now is to keep his core leaders working together and unified. He preaches constant communication. He SELLS constant communication. And we have bought what he's selling.

This book is a big sale too. It's selling you on the fact that you can be a leader. We are selling you the message that we have grown into leaders. We were not born leaders.

This book is ultimately selling you on what we believe to be true: that you can be an entrepreneur. If you have been in the military, then you have a head start. If you have not been in the military, then you'll have to work harder to learn the lessons in this book.

Bottom line: This book is selling you to you. Go out and take action. The world needs entrepreneurs.

– Robb LeCount

About the Author
Robert Kiyosaki

Best known as the author of *Rich Dad Poor Dad*—the #1 personal finance book of all time—Robert Kiyosaki has challenged and changed the way tens of millions of people around the world think about money. He is an entrepreneur, educator, and investor who believes the world needs more entrepreneurs who will create jobs.

With perspectives on money and investing that often contradict conventional wisdom, Robert has earned an international reputation for straight talk, irreverence, and courage and has become a passionate and outspoken advocate for financial education.

Robert and Kim Kiyosaki are founders of The Rich Dad Company, a financial education company, and creators of the *CASHFLOW*® games. In 2014, the company will leverage the global success of the Rich Dad games in the launch of a new and breakthrough offering in mobile and online gaming.

Robert has been heralded as a visionary who has a gift for simplifying complex concepts—ideas related to money, investing, finance, and economics—and has shared his personal journey to financial freedom in ways that resonate with audiences of all ages and backgrounds. His core principles and messages—like "your house is not an asset" and "invest for cash flow" and "savers are losers"—have ignited a firestorm of criticism and ridicule... only to have played out on the world economic stage over the past decade in ways that were both unsettling and prophetic.

His point of view is that "old" advice—go to college, get a good job, save money, get out of debt, invest for the long term, and diversify—has become obsolete advice in today's fast-paced Information Age. His Rich Dad philosophies and messages challenge the status quo. His teachings encourage people to become financially educated and to take an active role in investing for their future.

The author of 19 books, including the international blockbuster *Rich Dad Poor Dad*, Robert has been a featured guest with media outlets in every corner of the world— from CNN, the BBC, Fox News, Al Jazeera, GBTV and PBS, to *Larry King Live, Oprah, Peoples Daily, Sydney Morning Herald, The Doctors, Straits Times, Bloomberg, NPR, USA TODAY*, and hundreds of others—and his books have topped international bestsellers lists for more than a decade. He continues to teach and inspire audiences around the world.

His most recent books include *Unfair Advantage: The Power of Financial Education, Midas Touch*, the second book he has co-authored with Donald Trump, *Why "A" Students Work for "C" Students*, and *Second Chance*.

To learn more, visit RichDad.com

Bonus Section

Why I Asked Dave Leong to Write About the Honor Code

You might be surprised to learn how often we talk about Code, Code of Honor and Honor Code at The Rich Dad Company. When we do, I pull in Dave Leong and ask him to relate his experience with the Air Force and the Honor Code.

At Rich Dad we have a Code of Honor for our company and our partners. We encourage our employees to implement similar honor codes in their own businesses and business relationships. We even suggest that they establish a Code within their families, as Kim and I have done. It's a standard that we hold ourselves to and to which, when we commit to it, we are accountable.

It's not always easy to live by the Code, live with the outcomes when you or others violate its principles, but one thing is crystal clear: When there's a Code in place, you always know where you stand, what's expected of you, and what you can expect of others.

Dave tells us about his experiences in the Air Force with the Honor Code and how it shaped his perspective as he ventured out on his own with businesses and investments.

Thank you, Dave.

– Robert Kiyosaki

HONOR CODE

by Dave Leong

When Robert came to me and asked if I'd write a short piece on my experiences as a United States Air Force Academy graduate, I was caught a bit off guard—honored and slightly horrified, all at the same time. I'm a private person. I'm not an author.

However, in my time with Robert at The Rich Dad Company there has been one message that has always resonated with me: with change comes growth. So, here we go.

Robert specifically asked that I write about the Honor Code I lived and served under during my time at the Air Force Academy and while on active duty in the Air Force and how I'm applying it to my life as an aspiring entrepreneur and investor.

To get started, The United States Air Force Academy's Honor Code was: "We will not lie, steal, or cheat, nor tolerate among us anyone who does."

Each of the military academies—Air Force Academy, Naval Academy, Military Academy at West Point, and even the Merchant Marine Academy—maintains an Honor Code. State colleges and universities, even private ones, do not.

Honestly, I could bore you with a lot of my first-world problems at the academy and how living with an Honor Code as a knuckleheaded "college" student was a challenge. The genius behind an honor code or code of conduct, whether it's at a military academy, while on active duty, in a company on the civilian side, or in your own business, is that it takes the person out of the situation and it provides permission. It provides everyone within the organization permission to call out his or her co-workers and leadership. It takes the individual or personal aspect out of the issue and makes it about upholding the code—putting the organization first. Sound familiar?

I will relay one small, yet significant, experience I had while I was there that helped to shape me as a person working to provide value to this big world:

After putting in over three years of hard work, study, and discipline, we were finally in our 1st Degree (senior) year at The Zoo (an affectionate moniker for the academy). A few of my friends and I had a special affinity for sport bikes. We loved the sleek, sexy lines of the Ducati, Suzuki, and Honda motorcycles. The smell of the exhaust, the sheer amount of torque coming off the line, the handling around the curves, and the top-end speed proved too much of an allure for these four college students with some disposable cash.

The problem was The Zoo had a policy that restricted cadets from owning a motorcycle. Feeling a little too untouchable, we bought them anyway and stashed them at a friend's apartment (also not allowed). What could possibly go wrong?

As it turned out, a few months later our friend with the apartment and his soon-to-be-ex girlfriend had an alcohol-induced shouting match. It was loud enough that the police were called. Once it was discovered that he was a cadet, the local police contacted AFOSI (Air Force Office of Special Investigations). Think FBI.

The now-ex girlfriend made sure to let AFOSI know that other cadets (us) kept motorcycles at the apartment. She knew the potential repercussions. But, then again, so did we.

AFOSI was surgical in its precision in getting to each one of us separately. Even if we wanted to work on an alibi, we wouldn't have been able to.

It didn't matter. While we weren't completely straight-laced and knowingly broke some of the rules, we held to the Honor Code. No one denied what he did.

My best friend, and roommate, was interrogated. While he didn't own a motorcycle, he obviously knew whether *I* did or not. He cooperated and told the truth. He didn't feel great about it because he knew what it could mean for me. I appreciated why he felt that way, but I'd have been pissed at him if he didn't tell the truth. I expected him to tell the truth.

He was asked pointed questions and he gave truthful answers. We both signed up to abide by the Honor Code, and that's exactly what we did. No hard feelings. None.

At that point, it wasn't about him or me. It's only about the Honor Code and whether or not we followed it.

This all went down a scant three months before we were to graduate. The implication of our decision to own a motorcycle had the potential to be huge. If the Commandant of Cadets, a Colonel, so chose, we wouldn't be allowed to graduate, we would be kicked out of The Zoo, and then we'd serve our commitment as part of the Enlisted corps.

With those kinds of consequences at stake, the motivation to lie would be high for a lot of people, whether you're at The Zoo or a normal college. In the end, that didn't factor though. We decided to be men, took responsibility, and maintained our integrity.

While the process wasn't fun and the very real possibility of getting kicked out hung over our heads for four weeks, we still had the opportunity to graduate. If any of us had not adhered to the Honor Code and lied, we would have been gone in an instant.

To reiterate, having a code takes the person, ego, and emotion out of the situation. It sets the standard by which everyone is accountable and enables every single person in an organization, from the secretary to the president, to call out someone who isn't following the code.

The Honor Code made it that much easier for us to operate in the environment at The Zoo and uphold a standard. While "honor code" sounds stodgy and uptight, it provided everyone who agreed to follow it a standard. Call it whatever you want, but the code has to be known and adhered to by you as the business owner, your employees, and any outside firms, consultants, or advisers that you work with. Without a code, you're asking for chaos.

During my time at The Rich Dad Company as well as my efforts to get my business ideas off the ground, it's been of utmost importance to me that I create an atmosphere where I attract the right people with the right attitude. To ensure I achieve and maintain that atmosphere, I must know what's important to my business and what code I want my business, and everyone around it, to operate under. Nothing will disintegrate a good working environment faster than one where not everyone is held to the same standard or set of rules.

The Honor Code is something that every single person at The Zoo agreed to follow. Even though it only consisted of 14 words, it provided the structure to The Zoo and how the cadets operated within it. I, as all veterans, experienced a similar environment while on active duty. Now, I'm working to provide the code and structure for my own businesses.

There are reasons why young kids seek out the military: Discipline, code, honor, and a sense of being a part of something greater than themselves. Bring those same things with you to the civilian sector. They are wanted. And they're needed.

Veterans' knowledge base and ability to incorporate a code, an honor code, and a sense of mission are incredible assets as you begin on your road to becoming an entrepreneur.

An honor code isn't something you frame and put on a wall. It's part of a culture that demands a higher standard. It must be a culture that every member of the organization signs up for—*willingly!* Having lived and breathed it as a military veteran, it's a culture that you are capable of establishing and cultivating.

Special Report: VA Loans

SPECIAL REPORT
ON V.A. LOAN BENEFITS

Lessons in Life

During the time I served as a U.S. Marine I learned a lot about myself, about life, and about what was important in life. And I have to admit that some of these lessons took me decades to understand and appreciate. It was just this past year that I attended a reunion of my old platoon and apologized for my actions and my failure to always put the platoon first.

However, this special section isn't about me or my past. It's about how to take what I've learned about money and success and apply it to one of the greatest investing opportunity tools there is: the V.A. loan.

Rich or Poor

I often tell the story of my childhood. I had two fathers, a rich one and a poor one. One was highly educated and intelligent. He had a Ph.D. and completed four years of undergraduate work in less than two years. He then went on to Stanford University, the University of Chicago, and Northwestern University to do his advanced studies, all on full financial scholarships. The other father never finished the eighth grade.

Both men were successful in their careers, working hard all their lives. Both earned substantial incomes, yet one always struggled financially. One would become one of the richest men in Hawaii and leave tens of millions of dollars to his family, charities, and his church when he died. The other man left only bills that needed to be paid.

One of the reasons the rich get richer, the poor get poorer, and the middle class struggles with debt is that the subject of money is most often taught at home, not in school. Most of us learn about money from our parents. So what can poor parents teach their child about money? They simply say, "Stay in school and study hard so you can get a good job." The child may graduate with excellent grades, but with a poor person's financial programming and mind-set.

Sadly, the subject of money is rarely taught in schools. Schools focus on scholastic and professional skills, but not on financial skills. This explains how smart bankers, doctors, and accountants—who earned excellent grades in school—may struggle financially all of their lives. Our staggering national debt is due in large part to highly educated politicians and government officials making financial decisions with little or no training on the subject of money.

One dad, my poor dad, believed that a company or the government should take care of you and your needs. He was always concerned about pay raises, retirement plans, medical benefits, sick leave, vacation days, and other perks. He was impressed with two of his uncles who joined the military and earned a retirement-and-entitlement package for life after 20 years of active service. He loved the idea of the medical benefits and PX privileges the military provided its retirees. He also loved the tenure system available through the university. The idea of job protection for life and job benefits seemed more important, at times, than the job itself. He would often say, "I've worked hard for the government, and I'm entitled to these benefits."

Rich dad, on the other hand, believed in total financial self-reliance. He spoke out against the entitlement mentality and how it created weak, financially needy people. He was emphatic about being financially competent.

What's interesting to me is that the father who started poor and became a billionaire, my rich rad, also encouraged me to go into the military. Both fathers saw value in the military—but for very different reasons. While my poor dad valued the safe secure job, the retirement benefits, medical benefits, and vacation perks, my rich dad saw the value of leadership and team-building skills.

In the end, the reality is that the military, specifically the V.A. benefits, helped both men's view of the world become attainable. I just had to decide… did I want to be rich or poor?

Rich Dad Principles

On the Big Island of Hawaii, where I grew up, lies Parker Ranch. When I was in high school, Parker Ranch was the largest privately owned ranch in America. When I was 16 years old, rich dad took his son and me to visit the ranch. Far from the crowds and commercialism of Waikiki Beach, the ranch encompasses tall mountains, rolling green hills, and large expanses of land that reach out to the spectacular blue waters of the Pacific Ocean. Today, the little town of Kamuela, at the heart of the ranch, is a place I often dream of living one day.

On our visit to the ranch, we saw cowboys herding cattle from the feed yard to the slaughterhouse. Although rich dad took us away before we could see any cattle being slaughtered, we knew what was going to happen, and so did the cattle. It was an experience I will never forget.

A few months later, rich dad took us to a dairy farm. Early in the morning, we saw the farmer herding his cows into the barn for milking. These cattle behaved very differently.

The financial lesson rich dad wanted us to learn was that, while both the cattle rancher and the dairy farmer counted their cattle as assets, they treated those assets differently, and operated via different business models.

The visits to the ranch and the farm were meant to emphasize the very important difference between *capital gains* and *cash flow*

Simply put, a cattle rancher can be compared to a person who invests for capital gains. A dairy farmer is more like an investor who invests for cash flow.

One of the reasons so many people lose so much money investing, or think that investing is risky, is because they invest like ranchers. They invest to slaughter rather than to milk.

The Greatest of Fools

Besides greed and corruption, one of the primary reasons many people lose so much money investing is because they are investing for capital gains. During the tech bubble, it became so bad that investors were investing in companies that reported no earnings or profits, much less dividends. At the peak of the bubble, the fast money moved out and the greatest of fools emerged. Is this still going on today? Absolutely.

A Very Important Distinction

Whenever I hear someone say "Invest for the long term," I often ask, "What are you investing for? Are you investing for capital gains or for cash flow?" If I am investing for cash flow, I really do not care about price. I'll pay the price if I get cash flow—my return of my money now, not tomorrow, not in the long term. In other words, "Show me the money—now."

A Ridiculous Example

Here's a question: If you gave me $10 today, and I gave you back $1 a month for years, would you think that was a good investment? I hope you do. In this example, you would have your $10 back in ten months. From then on, it's free money.

One of the reasons many investors lose so much money is because they pay $10 a month into a fund for 40 years and don't know if it will be there 40 years from now. That is what I call "re-parking your money." Most likely there will be *something* there, but how much? And will it be enough?

I can hear some of you saying, "That example of investing $10 and getting back one dollar a month is a ridiculous example." Let me assure you, the example is not ridiculous. Since most people have been trained to invest for capital gains, they often fail to see the power of investing for cash flow.

The Slaughterhouse Mentality

One of the reasons rich dad took his son and me to both a ranch and a dairy farm was because he wanted to teach us the difference between slaughtering and milking. He often said, "When someone says they made a killing in the market, they really did. Some poor investor got killed. The slow investor lost, and the fast money got out. It happens all the time, and in all markets, not just the stock market."

Investing for Capital Gains Is Gambling

Anytime you invest with the hope of something (good) happening in the future, you are gambling. And that's what investing for capital gains is. I'm not saying that it's wrong. We should just see it for what it is and if it supports your investment goals.

Betting on the Super Bowl

Investing for capital gains is like betting at the start of the football season on which team will win the Super Bowl. In fact, it would probably be less risky make that crazy Super Bowl bet (before the season starts) than to invest for capital gains. Why? Because there aren't that many teams in the National Football League. There are thousands of stocks or mutual funds to choose from.

Rather than teach me to slaughter my assets, rich dad taught me to grow my assets by using cash flow to increase the size of my herd. Rather than take the cows to market, each year the cows have more calves… and the cash flow increases.

Cash flow is the key to financial success. It's the basis of our investing strategy and it's something I know a good bit about. What I'm not an expert at is V.A. loans.

On that subject, my friend and fellow veteran (although he was only a Navy man) Robb LeCount has taken the lead. He volunteered to meet regularly with one of our Rich Dad coaches and learn more about the benefits of the V.A. loan. Here's his Report.

– Robert Kiyosaki

Robb LeCount Reports

While Robert is right—that I am a proud Navy veteran—I think this might be the right time to remind Robert what Marine stands for: My Ass Rides In Navy Equipment. It has also been stated that Marine can stand for: Muscles Are Required Intelligence Not Essential.

Now, let's discuss V.A. Loans…

What Is a V.A. Loan?

Before we discuss how to turn your V.A. loan into a cash-flowing asset, we'll want to explain and understand what a V.A. loan is.

Very simply, every veteran has what's called a Certificate of Eligibility or COE. A COE is basically the V.A. guaranteeing each veteran a home loan. Because of this guarantee, your credit worthiness isn't a factor like it is with conventional home loans. You're able to buy a manufactured home, single-family home, a condominium… or a duplex, triplex, or four-plex, as long as it will be owner-occupied. You can even use your benefits to build a home.

In addition, because your loan is guaranteed, you do not have to pay private mortgage insurance (PMI). PMI is basically an imposed insurance policy that the conventional lenders will have you take out and that is for their benefit, not yours. Typically, a bank will require you pay for this PMI—which protects them, the bank. The PMI insurance is on top of your typical mortgage payment of principal, interest, taxes, and insurance. A V.A. loan does not require this because if a veteran were to default, the V.A. guarantees the lender that they will be made whole. Bottom line on this: If you have a V.A. loan, you won't be paying PMI.

Who Qualifies for a V.A. Loan?

Basically, every vet who is honorably discharged is eligible for the V.A. loan benefit. This applies to active duty, National Guard or reservists as well, in any branch of the military.

And lenders are not looking at your "qualifications" in the way a conventional underwriter does. They are not taking your pay grade into consideration or put you under extreme scrutiny.

One final point: you do not ever lose your benefits. If you've served in World War II, you would still have your COE. A lot of V.A. benefits can even pass on to spouses, so if certain requirements are met.

How V.A. Loans Are Used

The most common way V.A. loans are used is to buy a home. You can go out and buy your dream home and move in. You can also purchase a home in need of renovation or upgrades, especially energy efficient upgrades, and roll those repair and upgrade costs into your V.A. loan.

The next most common use of V.A. loan benefits is to refinance an existing mortgage. Since, basically, it's the property that is being 'qualified,' the process is that a V.A.-licensed appraiser would go out and make sure that the property meets minimum requirements; nothing too stringent. The sellers of the property may have to agree to pay some additional closing costs for the V.A. funding.

If you are refinancing and getting a better interest rate, the process is even easier. It's called an interest rate reduction refinance loan (IRRRL). What makes this loan great is that no appraisal is required. Your income and credit history are not even take into account. A IRRRL is about as easy as it gets.

Uncommon Ways to Use Your V.A. Benefits

There are also some less common and creative ways that V.A. loans can be used. When you purchase a home with your V.A. loan, the V.A. loan can be an asset, a bargaining chip, when you decide to sell your home. Your loan benefits get transferred to the new buyer. They can keep the interest rate and they get to keep the V.A. as the guarantor on the loan. This means that you can sell to people who might have trouble qualifying for a property or for a mortgage. Your pool of potential buyers is greater, just by having a V.A. loan on the property.

Another important thing to understand about your V.A. loan is that it can be used multiple times. It isn't there to use only one time on one house. If you have a V.A. loan for $400,000 and you use $200,000 to buy a house, you still have the remaining $200,000 to buy another house. There are rules that apply, of course, but it's something you should be aware of. Basically, you must live in your house for one year. What this means is you can buy two houses, each at $200,000—but you have to stretch out the purchases over two years. I guess this begs the question: Why would you want two houses? I'll put on my Rich Dad had to answer this: The second house is for investing purposes—whether you invest like a slaughterhouse or a dairy farmer.

My favorite way to use a V.A. loan is to buy a four-plex. I'm looking at buying one right now. I've found a four-plex for $200,000. My plan is to move my family into one of the units and rent out the other three. It's a formula for instant cash flow.

Robert's favorite area of the V.A. loan is the refinance benefit. V.A. loans allow you to do a cash-out refinance. A lot of banks with conventional loans discourage this. And the conventional banks that do permit it only do a cash-out refinance up to 80 or 85 percent of the total value of the house. With the V.A., you're able to go to 100 percent. So you may have bought your house for $150,000 using your COE a few years ago, and now you've paid off some of your principle and you have a $50,000 equity position in your property. As a vet, you'd be able to take full advantage of that equity with a cash-out refinance.

Why is this important? Let's say you've found another investment property to buy that needs a $20,000 down payment. You could pull out the $20,000 in a cash-out refinance and buy the new house. You now have another house that is using OPM (Other People's Money—in this case, your tenants) to pay down the mortgage AND generate monthly cash flow. In 15 to 30 years you will own the asset, and have generated a monthly cash flow. You've done all this thanks to your V.A. loan benefits. More good news: you can repeat this process and make huge strides in building your asset base and your wealth.

If you know anything about Robert's style of investing you know that cash flow is king—and that, in his opinion, investing for capital gains is gambling. Now that you've learned a bit about your V.A. loan, let's put the two concepts together.

V.A. Loan Meets Cash Flow Strategies

At Rich Dad we do not tell people what to do. We believe in getting educated and learning to make your best investment decisions for yourself.. We want to empower you, not command you. We can't expect to ever know everyone's personal situation, so for us to give advice would be wrong, foolish, and dangerous.

Instead of giving advice, allow me to show an example of how the V.A. loan benefits can work with the Rich Dad principle of cash flow to create success. Let's start our story with a veteran deciding to use his V.A. loan benefit of $400,000.

He knows he must buy a home, but he also wants the investment to cash flow. So he buys a $200,000 four-plex. His interest rate is 4 percent and his monthly mortgage payment is $1,200. He is able to rent the other three units at $700 a month each.

So each month he is collecting $2,100 in rent and paying out $1,200 in mortgage fees. Each month he has an initial surplus of $900. Keep in mind that this example uses easy-to-compute 'round numbers.' The $900 each month is *before* any other bills or repair and maintenance costs are deducted, but it's still a pretty good deal.

Our vet stays in his house for a full year, then does the exact same thing again. So now he has seven units paying $700 a month and he has a monthly mortgage payment of $2,400 (2 X $1,200). His profit is now $2,500 a month—$4,900 less $2,400! That's not too bad, is it? But he's not done yet. Our vet has his first property re-evaluated. The value in the house has gone up, partially because he bought in the right neighborhood, but also because the property is a proven asset. He is able to pull out $20,000 in a cash-out refinance.

Now our vet takes the $30,000 from the cash-out refinance, adds $10,000 from his own money—note that this is the first time he's had to use his own money, money that was his cash flow of $10,800 from his rental units in year one—and buys another four-plex for $200,000. The difference is that this loan is a conventional loan because he had already used all of his V.A. loan benefits.

The conventional loan is not as profitable. Now our vet must pay PMI insurance and his interest rate is higher. These four new units still rent for $700 each but his monthly mortgage payment is $1,500. The monthly cash flow for these units is $1,300 ($2,800 - $1,500).

After 12 months, our vet now owns eight units using his V.A. loan benefits, netting him $2,500 a month *plus* 4 more units through a conventional loan netting him $1,300 a month. That's a total of $3,800 a month. And this is after just one year!

If you can assume our veteran saves his new-found cash flow from the year, it would mean he has $45,600 in the bank. What does he do next? He takes the $35,000 from the cash-out refinance of both four-plexes and buys two more four-plexes for $200,000 each with conventional loans. Even though he is now using conventional loans, this is only possible because of the cash-out refinance benefit from the V.A. loans. These two new properties add another $2,600 to his cash flow each month.

In this perfect-world scenario, our vet is making $6,400 a month in passive income. Passive income is income you earn whether you are working or not. Our vet now has choices to make. He can sit back and do nothing and enjoy life… or he can follow this path toward greater wealth. He is in control and can determine what he wants to do with his life. And because his income surpasses his expenses, he is financially free.

Oh, yeah… and he pays almost nothing in taxes. I'll save that for my next Special Report.

Back to you, Marine.

Robert's Closing Thoughts
Take Action!

Everyone has been given two great gifts: your mind and your time. The military has given you a third, your V.A. loan. It's up to you to do what you please with all three.

With each dollar of income you generate, you, and only you, have the power to determine your destiny. Spend it foolishly, and you choose to be poor. Invest it in your mind and learn how to acquire assets, and you will be choosing wealth as your goal and your future. The choice is yours, and only yours. Every day and with every dollar, you decide to be rich, poor, or middle class.

Veterans also have dollars that you don't even see. Your V.A. loan benefits represent hundreds of thousands of dollars. Make wise, cash-flowing choices and you will see success. I encourage you to see your V.A. loan as a tool, a weapon against poverty and your path to financial freedom.

Your future, and the future of your family, will be determined by choices you make today, not tomorrow.

I wish you great wealth and much happiness with this fabulous gift called life.

– Robert Kiyosaki

An Excerpt from

★ ★ ★ ★ ★

Why We Want You To Be Rich

by
Donald J. Trump and
Robert T. Kiyosaki

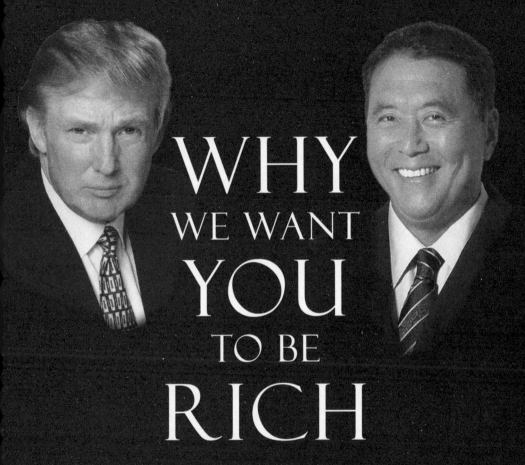

WHY
WE WANT
YOU
TO BE
RICH

TWO MEN • ONE MESSAGE

DONALD J.
TRUMP | KIYOSAKI
ROBERT T.

HOW DID MILITARY SCHOOL HELP DEFINE YOUR LIFE?

Robert's Response

There are three reasons I went to a military school.

When I was 10 years old, my fifth-grade teacher had us study the history of the great explorers—Columbus, Cortez, Magellan and Da Gama. Reading those books inspired me to want to go to sea and explore the world.

When I was 13, while other kids were carving salad bowls for their moms, I talked my shop teacher into letting me build a boat for my wood shop project. I sent away for the plans and for the next few months, I was happily building an 8-foot El Toro class sailboat. That class was one of the few classes I got an A in.

Some of the happiest days of my life were spent sailing my boat on Hilo Bay, named after the town I grew up in. As I sat in my boat, my mind would drift as I dreamed of faraway ports and exotic women.

When my high school guidance counselor asked me, "What do you want to do when you grow up?" I replied, "I want to go to sea, travel to exotic places such as Tahiti, drink beer and chase women."

Instead of getting upset with me, she said, "I have just the school for you." She then took out a brochure for the U.S. Merchant Marine Academy and said, "Look this over. It's a tough school. But if you really want to go to sea, then I'll help you get into the academy."

After winning a congressional appointment from U.S. Senator Daniel K. Inouye in 1965, I left the sleepy little town of Hilo and traveled to New York to begin my education to become a merchant marine officer. In 1968, as part of my apprenticeship at sea, I sailed

...I realized that combat was the ultimate test of will and training. There was no second place and the winner was the one who was the most prepared.

I changed my thoughts to, "Combat is not risky. Being unprepared is risky." I've come to realize that entrepreneurship is not risky. Being unprepared is risky.

– Robert T. Kiyosaki

into Papaete, Tahiti, drank beer, and went out with one of the most beautiful women I have ever met. She was the weather girl on television and a candidate for Miss Tahiti. My dreams had come true.

The second reason I went to the academy was because my dad did not have the money to send me to college. He said to me, "The day you graduate, you are on your own." And I was. Going to the academy meant I had a full scholarship, room, board and clothing allowance, and reimbursement for travel. On top of that, we were paid a small (and I do mean small) salary each month.

The third, and probably the most important reason, was for the discipline. As a kid in high school, I was often surfing more than attending class. Even after my dad, the head of education, caught me, I still found it impossible not to cut classes when the surf was big.

I knew I needed the discipline. If I had attended the University of Hawaii, I never would have finished school.

At the academy, I learned discipline... the hard way. Punishment came often, and it was severe. Academics were tougher than I had expected. Without a strict military system, I would never have graduated.

I also learned to follow and give orders. In other words, I learned leadership. When you look at the CASHFLOW Quadrant, you can see that leadership is essential for success in the B quadrant. After three years of hard discipline and leadership training, in my senior year, I was promoted to Battalion Officer. My job was then to teach leadership to underclassmen who were just like me when I entered the school—little con artists who thought they could beat the system.

The Biggest Lessons of All

After four years of the academy, I volunteered for the Marine Corps because the Vietnam War was still going. It was in Navy flight school that I had two life-defining lessons that have served me well. They are:

1. One of the most exciting parts of flight training was learning how to fight aircraft to aircraft, often called a dogfight. The aircraft we flew at the time was a T-28 Trojan, a single-engine World War II vintage aircraft. It was big, fast and unforgiving. Many a student died because the aircraft was designed to be agile and maneuverable. If you were not a good pilot, the aircraft could kill you.

   One day, I was flying solo, on the lookout for my instructor who was going to jump me. Suddenly, I heard screaming through my helmet's earpiece: "Bang, bang, bang, bang!" It was the instructor letting me know the fight was on. Immediately, I did as I was taught, shoving the fuel mixture to rich to protect the engine and pulling the aircraft up to the right and rolling it over, trying to shake my attacker.

   Instead of losing him, all I could hear was, "Bang, bang, bang, got you, sucker." I could not shake my instructor. I climbed, I turned, I dove, I tried to stall, but nothing could shake him. I could barely see because my face shield was covered in sweat. For a good 10 minutes, my instructor rode my tail, not fooled by any of my evasive maneuvers.

   Back on the ground, the debriefing began. As my instructor used his hands to describe my flying, I got sick to my stomach. My ill feeling was not just because of the violent maneuvers we had just been through. It was the realization of how bad a pilot I was and how much more I had to learn.

   At that moment, my instructor said something that has stayed with me ever since: "The trouble with this business is that there is no second place. Only one pilot comes home alive." That was a defining moment in my life. After that day, I practiced and practiced and practiced.

Later in Vietnam, I would hear those same words several times. Only this time, it was for real. There were real bullets. Not my instructor screaming "bang, bang, bang" over his radio.

I win in business today not because I am smart or never fail. I win because, in my world, there is no second place. I suspect Donald has the same personal rule.

2. The other defining moment pertains to risk.

Whenever I hear someone say, "Investing is risky," I know it really means the person is not prepared and is not up to the task.

After that day in the air with my flight instructor, I realized that combat was the ultimate test of will and training. There was no second place and the winner was the one who was the most prepared. I changed my thoughts to, "Combat is not risky. Being unprepared is risky."

In business and investing, I am a fanatic about practice and preparation. I practice to reduce risk. I improve my skills to reduce risk. I study to reduce risk. I play to win, and the prize goes to the one who plays the game with the least risk and the most confidence.

If I need to take a risk, I take a small one. Before I invested with real money in my first real estate deal, I attended a workshop for investors. Following that workshop, I looked at over a hundred deals. Everywhere I went in Hawaii, realtors kept saying, "What you're looking for doesn't exist." After months of looking, I finally found a small deal on the island of Maui. It was a one-bedroom condominium, near the beach, for only $18,000. It was my first investment. Since then, I have looked at tens of thousands of possible investments and purchased only a few of them.

After losing my nylon surfer-wallet business, I went back to the discipline of study, practice, study, practice. I realized that entrepreneurship is not risky. Being unprepared is risky.

Understanding that, in my world, there is no second place and realizing that the biggest risk is being unprepared have made the biggest differences in my quest for wealth.

Most people invest money and do not invest much time. Donald and I invest a lot of time before we invest much money. We prepare to invest. I realized that entrepreneurship is not risky. Being unprepared is risky.

Military School vs. Business School

When you look at the B-I Triangle, it is easy to see why military school and military service are great preparation for entrepreneurship and investing. Simply put, business schools focus on the inside of the B-I triangle... the content. Military schools focus on the outside... the context.

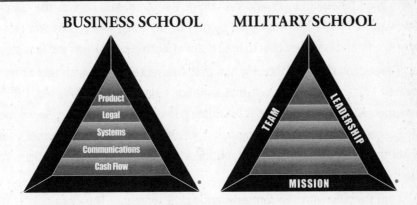

As you can tell from the diagram, four years of military school and nearly six years in military service prepared me for the real world of entrepreneurship and investing. It was a great education because the process taught me: 1. Discipline 2. Focus. 3. To serve a mission greater than my own self-interests. 4. To take orders, follow orders, and give orders. 5. To control my fears and my anger 6. To study and respect my enemy. 7. To trust my fellow soldiers and be willing to give my life for them as they were willing to give their lives for me. 8. To prepare before going into battle.

Donald's Response

Although I was sent to military school because I was a bit aggressive as a kid, what I learned there had less to do with discipline and channeling my energy more effectively than it had to do with learning about the art of negotiation. It was a great business lesson in disguise.

I was confronted with a former marine drill sergeant, and I realized I would never be able to match him or take him on physically, so I had to use my brain to handle the situation.

I had to get around the guy somehow, and I refused to back down, so I tried to figure out what might get him on my side. I saw my first opportunity: I was a very good baseball player and captain of the team, and he was the coach. I knew I could make him look good by playing my best, which I did. We had a great team, and I learned how to lead them effectively. That was the first step.

The second step was showing him that I respected him (which wasn't hard because I did respect him), but that I wouldn't let him intimidate me. I think he respected that and realized it would be pointless to go after me. So we met each other from a point of strength, not weakness, and a mutual respect was established. That's another great business lesson right there, especially for negotiation. We both won.

I am friendly with the former marine drill sergeant, Theodore Dobias, to this day, and meeting up with him at the New York Military Academy was a fortunate event for me. So was going to military school, although I wasn't that thrilled about it initially. I later realized that I enjoyed the challenges and the discipline, and I never lost the respect for time that I learned there. People who know me know that I hate being late, and I don't like other people being late either.

Military school underscored what my father had always taught us—that we should show respect. I respected Mr. Dobias and it served me well, and I learned to respect time, which has also served me well. My father was a real taskmaster as a businessman and I was ready to work with him after that training.

Another important lesson from military school was that excuses aren't acceptable. You learn not to whine, but instead to keep your equilibrium and persevere. When I faced difficulties and pressures later in life, I refused to cave in. I knew that the best way to deal with problems was to just keep going, to persist and continue working at solutions. That's a good lesson to learn.

While I was in military school, my father got into the habit of sending me inspirational quotes each week. I can remember a lot of them and they continue to inspire me today. A few of them are:

"He who has never learned to obey cannot be a good commander."

— Aristotle

"Never tell people how to do things. Tell them what to do and they will surprise you with their ingenuity."

— George S. Patton

"What you cannot enforce, do not command."

— Sophocles

"We are what we repeatedly do. Excellence then is not an act, but a habit."

— Aristotle

I realize my father was instilling leadership values in me by selecting certain bits of wisdom from many ages. These lessons went into my subconscious, surfacing to help me as I encounter situations that they might pertain to. That's why I'm still big on quotes; they can be a direct hit on negative or confused thinking. So when people hear me quoting or referring to a variety of great thinkers throughout history, they now know it's something that was started at a young age and that I have continued to do. And it started when I was in military school.

Another defining moment I had in military school had to do with history. There was a fellow student who was always studying WWII on his own. He was a history buff and a serious student. One day I said to him, "You must be an expert on WWII after all the time you've spent studying it." His reply is something I've never forgotten: "No, it has only made me realize how much I don't know." Then he explained that in order to understand WWII, he had to go back to WWI and study that, and then study the world situation before WWI, and he was beginning to see it would be a very long process. Then he said, "Studying history has made me very humble, because I know I'll never know it all." Coming from someone as well-read as he was, those comments left an impression on me.

As a result, I would study history in my spare time and try to read as much as I could. I started a habit that I've kept to this day, which is to ask myself, "What can I learn today that I didn't know before?" That's one way to keep my mind curious and alert. Aristotle was right: Excellence can become a habit.

When I entered Wharton years later, I found that my habits from military school helped me a great deal. As I mentioned earlier, I spent my spare time studying foreclosures and real estate and everything I could get my hands on —all in addition to the required curriculum. I didn't want to get by with just doing enough. I wanted to do more, and I found myself prepared when I left college for the real world where very often doing "enough" really isn't enough at all.

In the words of one of the Greek philosophers my father introduced me to, here's a final, defining lesson I learned at military school:

"The first and best victory is to conquer self."

— Plato

> The more you learn, the more you realize how much you don't know.
>
> *– Donald J. Trump*

I learned to be part of a whole. Military school provided the opportunity to understand how to be part of the big picture without losing my identity. It's been a great advantage in business, allowing me to diminish myself when necessary.

Sometimes the picture is clearer if you're not in the picture at all. A great lesson. Someone once said I was a bit like a chameleon when it came to negotiating, that I could blend myself out and then back in again. That ability came from my experiences at military school.

Most people see me as being mentally tough, and that's true. That's another advantage I've had from my time in military school. I don't like to complain, I can be tenacious, and sometimes I just won't budge. If I've done my homework, if I've worked hard and I've been diligent, then I know I have everything it takes to back myself up or defend myself. I can be a tough adversary.

As I said, I was sent to military school because I was a bit aggressive as a kid. In military school I learned to focus my aggressiveness for good instead of bad and became a leader as well as a member of a team with a common mission.

Robert at Camp Pendleton, California,
preparing to go to Vietnam, 1972.

Donald leading the New York Military
Academy contingent up Fifth Avenue
for the Columbus Day parade, 1963.

Your Response

What did you learn in military school that helped define your life?

You may not have attended military school, but did you belong to the Boy Scouts, Girl Scouts or other clubs where you learned the importance of discipline and leadership? How have you benefited from these experiences? Or, how could you have benefited from using self-discipline and leadership skills in your life?

_____

_____

_____

Where in your life could you benefit from more discipline (i.e., time management or financial management?) and/or more leadership skills?

_____

_____

_____

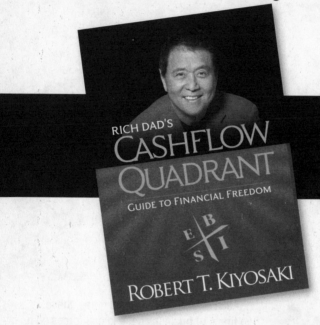

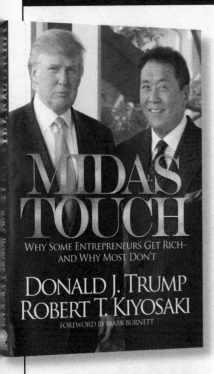

Bring Out the Rich Woman in You

Let's face it. When it comes to money, men and women are different. There are unique issues that women face when it comes to money and investing. And now there is a book on money uniquely for women.

Now is the time for women to get smarter with their money. Kim Kiyosaki's passion is to educate and encourage women to create financial security and peace of mind. That's why she wrote **Rich Woman.**

- Stop losing sleep over money.
- Take control of your financial future.
- Forget about looking for a rich Prince Charming.
- Demand true independence.

Start your journey to financial independence today.

"This book is a must-read for all women. Today, more than ever, women need to be financially savvy."   – Donald Trump

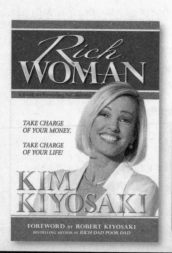

It's Rising Time! A new title, now available, from Kim.

Get your copy of *Rich Woman* **today!**

Order at **richwoman.com**

Notes

Notes